First Time Dad

The 42 Week Guide For Men To Help Your Partner Have A Calm & Confident Pregnancy

James Macdonald

Contents

This book is for Dad, who during his 70th birthday speech, said the best protection a man can have is his family and friends.

Introduction

My name is James, and after becoming a dad over a decade ago, I'm still a happily married father of three. In that we're all still here, mostly still sane, I'm doing an alright job.

In this book, I write about my experience of becoming a dad for the first time and what might happen in the world of you and your baby.

This book will update you week-to-week on your baby's developments. I also provide suggestions to help support your mental health and relationship.

Everyone's pregnancy experience is beautifully unique, but I'm confident there are enough universal truths to make this a worthwhile read for anyone.

I'm very much in the "trying to learn through mistakes and not make too many of the same ones again" school of thought.

Becoming a dad was and continues to be the most profoundly humbling experience of my life.

Watching your partner give birth is undoubtedly the most magical and surreal experience a person can have. It has ups and downs, but becoming a parent positively affects your life if you embrace it fully.

If someone has given you this book, then I assume you or they have just found out you're going to become a dad.

Congratulations, and I hope the news is more than 51% exciting rather than terrifying. If you are feeling mildly terrified, don't worry. That's a natural reaction for most men.

I had those feelings when my partner told me she was pregnant. In all honesty, a general sense of panic is one of my default settings for life as a dad.

I remember having significant self-doubt when my wife trusted me to look after our 3-week-old daughter for the first time.

We were on a routine family trip to the GP. The doctor had advised us to go to A and E immediately because my wife had an abscess that looked infected.

Dropping my wife off at the hospital left me alone with our 3-week-old daughter for the first time. Once we were safely home, I set up my "daddy day care" in the bedroom. I remember creating a moat of pillows around the bed just in case I passed out and my daughter—who couldn't support her head or roll at that point—suddenly learnt how to.

I had two mobile phones, a first aid kit and my mum's number on speed dial.

There hasn't been a week—okay, a day—since when I haven't doubted my ability to complete something parent related.

Unfortunately, your children won't come with a manual. If they did, it would be unreadable, missing pages, finger smudged and covered in *Peppa Pig* stickers.

If you're filled with self-doubt, remember that rubbish husbands or boyfriends don't buy, let alone read, books about how best to support themselves or their partners during pregnancy.

Therefore, you're probably already one of the good guys.

All the best and good luck,

James

Qualified Level 3 Dad

Chapter 1
Week 1

How Does Your Partner Know She's Pregnant?

The number one sign is that your partner's period hasn't arrived when she expects it. If you have been with your partner for a few months or longer, you may "sense" when it's her time of the month. This "sense" may also be what inspires you to move the knife block into the garage.

Survival Tip

If you suspect she's on her period, I wouldn't ask her if that's why she seems a bit irritable, irrational, or passive-aggressive.

What's A Period?

The "period" is the womb lining that appears once a month. Your partner's body is preparing for ovulation (releasing an egg from one of her ovaries).

A period won't arrive if the egg your partner's body produces gets fertilised by one of your sperm.

5 to 6 days after ovulation, her fertilised egg burrows into the lining of her womb (a process called implantation). She is now pregnant.

Congratulations!

For a woman not planning a pregnancy or believing she can't get pregnant, week one will sail past without her realising anything different. A lot of the symptoms (fatigue, mood swings, and the constant need to urinate) may be what she is used to experiencing during her monthly period.

She will know her body and when a period is en route better than anyone. Naturally, therefore, she'll be acutely aware of anything different. For example, in the second week, she may find cervical mucus in her underwear.

This is vaginal discharge that looks and feels slippery and stretchy, like raw eggs.

Your partner may also experience an increased sex drive, which should be more than enough evidence for any man to question something is different.

Women being the clear masterminds of our species, if she wants you to impregnate her, she'll probably manage just fine. In my case, there's a black low-cut top, a tomahawk steak, and the second bottle of merlot that has quite a lot to answer for!

Another giveaway sign that she might be pregnant is that she may have an increased basal body temperature.

My wife's hair and eyes were also noticeably different. In what way, I'm still determining; maybe brighter and a bit shinier.

I also remember one night, my wife seemed dangerously hot. I was convinced she had the flu. She agreed she was very hot but said she felt fine.

How Can You Support Your Partner, Baby & Yourself In Week 1?

In that you don't yet know she's pregnant, the best you can do is to continue being the loving and supportive husband or boyfriend I imagine you can be.

She may think it's her period making her tired and grumpy as opposed to being pregnant. I live by the idea that it's better to be kind than right and maybe buying the bigger bag of Maltesers.

If her mood triggers you and you can feel yourself getting cross or frustrated, create some physical distance. Go for a run, walk or win some serious brownie points by doing that DIY project she's still on about.

Chapter Takeaways

1. Continue to be the loving and supportive man you can be.
2. If you're frustrated or cross at her moodiness, put physical distance between you and go for a walk.
3. Go to a shop and buy her chocolate on the way back from your calming walk.

"Any man can be a father, but it takes someone special to be a dad."

- Anne Geddes, World Renowned Australian

Photographer

Chapter 2
Week 2

I'm Not Fond Of The Sight Of Blood Will I Manage To Watch The Birth?

As mentioned, the earliest and probably most reliable sign of pregnancy is that your partner has missed her period.

She may have a bleed in the first few weeks, which might seem very light. This is called "implantation bleeding."

Survival Tip

Without wanting to encourage a feminist wave of abuse, if, like me, the terms "implantation bleeding," "vaginal discharge," or "egg burrowing," can make you feel queasy or a bit repulsed by the whole thing, keep it to yourself.

(I'm obviously not saying repulsed by the idea of the birth of your child, which is a beautiful manifestation of the circle of life etc., more the internal plumbing and constant referencing to it.)

I was worried that when the time came to meet our daughter, I would end up a sweaty, pale mess on the floor in front of my partner and a team of disapproving midwives.

You'll be delighted to hear this very nearly happened during the birth of number two. You may be disappointed to hear I kept it together for the maiden voyage.

As someone with a form for ending up in a sweaty, fainty mess, you may surprise yourself when the time comes.

What's The Afterbirth?

Afterbirth is the term used to describe the placenta and foetal membranes pushed out after birth. It's best described as a pancake-shaped bag full of blood and other things that look like bodily belongings!

The placenta is impressive. It's an organ that is developed in the uterus exclusively during pregnancy. It provides your baby with water, oxygen, nutrients, and antibodies to fight disease. Doing my best not to sound like a letting agent; it also has its own waste-removal system.

It's the literal life force for your unborn child. In retrospect, it probably demands a more respectful description than my reaction of, "Wow, it's like a big bag of blood!"

How Can You Support Your Partner, Baby & Yourself In Week 2?

Your partner may still be blissfully unaware she's pregnant. She may also be experiencing a desire for new tastes and smells. My wife craved oranges and anything citrus with our first (our daughter) and coffee with our second and third (the boys). If she suddenly asks you to go and buy her some oranges at 8pm on a Sunday night, do it. The exercise will do you good, the show of support will do your relationship good, and the vitamin C will do her and your baby's immune system good.

Chapter Takeaways

1. If you're worried about fainting during childbirth, you have two options: explain your concerns to your partner and stay firmly at the head end.
2. Start learning about it. Understanding what's happening might help change your perception of it.

"What makes you a man is not the ability to make a child, it's the courage to raise one."

- Ex US President Barack Obama

Chapter 3
Week 3

What Can I Do To Support My Partner If Her Increased Sense Of Smell Makes Her Feel Sick?

At three weeks, your partner has officially conceived and is in her first month of pregnancy. In the third week, tiny clusters of cells that will become your baby are growing.

Your partner's surging hormone levels may cause her to have an increased sense of smell, which might help explain her new cravings or her feelings of sickness.

The pregnancy hormone HGC can cause anxiety, vomiting, nausea, light-headedness, fainting, dizziness, exhaustion, and mood swings. If that wasn't enough to deal with, her breasts could become increasingly tender and sore.

That said, it's not all bad; some medical journals described it as more of a tingling sensation than a tender and sore one.

Survival Tip

It might be wise not to vocalise any comments about breast-tingling sensations being considered a plus. I'm confident your pregnant partner won't share your views. She's probably feeling tired, sore, nauseous, and therefore devoid of gratitude.

What Is Morning Sickness & Why Is It Called That?

I'm assuming it got this name because women tend to feel nauseous earlier in the day. I don't know how much evidence, if any, there is to support this.

Your partner may start to feel some sickness at around the 4-to-6-week point. This is unhelpfully referred to as morning sickness, as anyone who has experienced it will tell you it can and will happen at any time day or flipping night.

How Can You Support Your Partner, Baby & Yourself In Week 3?

The hormonal changes your partner is experiencing can often make her tired, sick, and very emotional. If you can always bear that in mind and try to be kind and compassionate, that will reap rewards.

You may also be feeling more emotional, but you're not growing a baby, so you should probably keep quiet about that. This is a problematic issue as I think it should be more socially acceptable for soon-to-be dads to ask for support if they feel emotionally overwhelmed.

I tend to agree with the social consensus that, as a dad, you're not the priority here.

You may be disappointed if you're hoping for your partner to do the lion's share of this work and still look to manage your emotional and physical needs. That said, being aware of your mental health is very important, and many online groups for men can provide advice and support.

Overall, I felt excited about becoming a dad, but I did and still do have sleepless nights about how I will financially provide for my family.

I found a lot of support from friends and family members who were already dads. Talking to them helped answer many of my questions and dispel most of my anxieties.

By self-managing yourself and having the headspace to support your partner, you will create an environment where it's okay for her to admit her worries.

Chapter Takeaways

1. Avoid cooking overly fragrant food if your partner is nauseous. If you smoke, you may never get a better reason than this to kick the habit.
2. If she's very emotional, just be kind and compassionate. She's not asking you to fix her worries; just listen to them and be aware of them.
3. Now would be an excellent time to reach out to any of your friends who are dads. Having them to confide in over the next 9 months may be a massive help.

"Never is a man more of a man than when he is the father of a newborn."

- American Actor Matthew McConaughey

Chapter 4
Week 4

What Hormone Is My Partner's Body Producing?

In the 4th week, her body produces the pregnancy hormone HGC which is bossily telling her body not to throw away the lining of the uterus because, well, she's pregnant and needs it.

In weeks 4 and 5 of the pregnancy, the embryo will grow and develop within the womb lining.

Survival Tip

It may be tempting when people start mentioning hormones to tell a "*How do you make a hormone?*" joke. I certainly wouldn't do what one man did during our antenatal class.

During a break in the conversation, he quietened down the NCT lady and ashen-faced partner to loudly share his hormone joke.

In case you are wondering, his answer was: "*Don't pay her?*"

How Is Our Baby Developing At This Stage?

Outer cells reach out to form links to the blood supply, and inner cells form into two and three layers. Each layer is responsible for growing different parts of your baby's body.

The inner layer will grow into the breathing and digestive systems, which include the lungs, stomach, and bladder.

The middle layer will develop into the heart, blood vessels, muscles, and bones.

The embryo has a yolk sac in the first few weeks of pregnancy, a bit like a mini-packed lunch. If your baby had the ability to speak, it might be asking why it can't have a *Paw Patrol* lunch box like its brother or Walkers crisps like everyone else. Later, this yolk sac/mini-pack lunch will turn into the placenta.

What's The Placenta?

The placenta ensures the baby will receive the oxygen and nutrients it needs. If the placenta could talk, it might explain that the embryo has a *Paw Patrol* lunch box, but it's still stuck on the garage roof. It might also remind the embryo that regardless of the brand, crisps are meant for after-school clubs, not the 8am journey to school!

How Can You Support Your Partner, Baby & Yourself In Week 4?

You may notice that your partner needs the loo a lot more. This can be annoying if it causes you to be late to meet friends or watch a film, etc.

It's worth remembering that, as men, we will never truly understand the physical discomfort or emotional stress that accompanies being pregnant. I've had intrusive thoughts about catching life-threatening diseases from communal toilets in the past. If your partner's desire to find a pub with cleaner toilets adds time to your journey or means you miss the trailers, just breathe, go with it and remember that she is growing your son or daughter.

Chapter Takeaways

1. Increase patience and compassion and decrease any grumpiness about having to find a pub with cleaner toilets.
2. Her body produces a hormone called HGC, but save any hormone jokes for your workmates, not a room full of pregnant women.

3. Continue to take an interest in your child's development, and it will make you more emotionally engaged and probably earn you some brownie points.

"By the time a man realises that maybe his father was right, he usually has a son who thinks he's wrong."

- Classical Pianist Charles Wandsworth

Chapter 5
Week 5

How Big Is Our Baby Now?

Your baby's nervous system is already developing, and the foundations for its major organs are in place. At this stage, the embryo is around 2mm long, which is about the size of a baked bean or slightly bigger than your friend's penis if he mentions that you look a bit like a fat Richard Gere!

An enormous amount is happening inside your partner's body. The baby's heart will start as a simple tube-like structure, it has blood vessels, and the blood will begin to circulate. Over time a string of these blood vessels will connect your baby to your partner and become the umbilical cord.

Survival Tip

A solid sense of humour is the cannon in your war against stress and pregnancy angst, but it's all about timing. I can remember several occasions when I got it massively wrong. Still, there were times when a well-timed dad joke, usually at my expense, helped scatter her thunderclouds and reminded my partner that even though her husband was a bit of a clown, his heart was in the right place.

For example, we had fallen out while shopping for a present for a friend's 3-year-old, and she grumpily suggested some wooden Russian Dolls. My answer of, "I like Russian Dolls, but they can be so full of themselves!" seemed to defrost her mood slightly.

How Can You Support Your Partner, Baby & Yourself In Week 5?

This is the time of the first missed period. If her raging heat in bed or the rare scenario of her finding you attractive wasn't a giveaway, she might also start to suspect she's pregnant.

At 5 weeks, your partner may feel constipated and have vaginal discharge but vaginal discharge without soreness or irritation. Again, in these early stages, it's essential to be kind and patient with your partner. There is so much change going on, and if this is her first pregnancy, there may be increased anxiety about the future.

If you can tell she's worried but also trying to put on a brave face, don't be scared to rock the boat and ask how she is. If you get a non-committal "I'm fine!" when she's anything but, dare to push her until you get the truth. You may get shouted at, there may be tears, and she may throw several scatter cushions but having the strength to face up and deal with all of this will serve two purposes.

Firstly, it will reassure her that not only are you someone who won't run when times are tough, but you're mentally strong enough for both of you—sorry, all three of you!

Secondly, it will also show *you* the reserves of mental strength you may never have realised were there until a unique life experience like this uncovers them. You displaying to your partner that you're capable of dealing with her emotionally-driven verbal barbs and scatter cushions will empower you.

Being more of a man will give her the licence to be more of a woman and will show her that you have this whole becoming-a-family gig under control.

How Can You Confirm If She's Pregnant?

The following depends on if your partner ever goes shopping with my wife's friend Jacky.

Stage 1) You meet Jacky in H&M to look at denim jackets, and before she says anything else, she comments, "Your boobs look massive. I bet you're pregnant!"

Stage 2) She frog marches you into Superdrug, and you buy, I imagine, their stock of pregnancy tests.

What Is A Pregnancy Test?

It's a mini chemistry set that's luckily cheap enough if she can't use the first test she dropped on the toilet floor—even if it was caught by her knickers' safety net—she can buy another.

The test can detect if there is a hormone called HCG (*Human Chorionic Gonadotrophin*) in her pee. It looks a bit like a Covid Test (*I couldn't have written this in 2019*). The urine seeps up the dipstick on the test, passing through a layer containing antibodies that stick to the HCG hormone. It will give a positive reading if this hormone is present in her pee. The most common available brand seems to be Clear Blue, which I suppose makes sense because if she is pregnant, the kit will indicate this by showing a blue (+) or the word (*POSITIVE*) in the result window.

If the window shows a (-), she is not pregnant. These tests are 97% accurate; some are so sensitive that they can detect changes in her hormones the day her period is due.

The third and final stage is for your partner to make an appointment to see her GP. The primary purpose being so they can enter her details into the NHS antenatal system. What is this? Well, her GP needs to enter her details into this system to ensure her appointments, ultrasound scans, and a care plan that is specific to her health needs can be set up. If your partner still needs to get signed up with a local GP, now is the time to get that done.

If she can't get an appointment straight away...don't panic; it's all good. It won't make much difference if she sees the GP at 5 weeks pregnant or 8 weeks pregnant. The only situation where this is different is if:

- She has a pre-existing health problem
- She has a history of miscarriage
- She thinks she's further along, 10 or more weeks

If your partner remembers to mention all this information on the phone, she will be supported accordingly.

Will Her GP Do Another Pregnancy Test?

No, the GP will take you at your word, as the home tests are considered accurate. Your GP doesn't have a secret stash of

97% to 100% tests for the wives of Navy SEALs, superheroes, or mythical creatures.

So What Happens Then?

I just asked my wife this, which, yes, I suppose could indicate that sometimes I don't listen to "Absolutely everything, darling!"

1. The GP establishes the date of your partner's last period.
2. The GP advises what to eat and what not to eat, for example avoiding alcohol, seafood, and soft cheese.
3. She advises starting to take folic acid straight away. Folic acid is the synthetic version of the vitamin folate known as vitamin B9. Folate helps the body to make healthy blood cells. It's more relevant now as it will allow the baby's brain, skull, and spinal cord to develop properly.
4. The GP will pass on Mum's details to the local midwife service team, who will then contact her regarding appointments and scans. The midwife team will get her to arrange an appointment at around 10 weeks. The scans are at 12 weeks and 20 weeks.
5. Your GP may take her blood pressure.

How & When Might She Break The Exciting News to You, The Father?

I got a phone call while waiting for a train to take me back to Brighton. I had taken my mum to the West End to see a performance of The Lion King. I may well have been grumbling about the cost of laughably small tubs of vanilla ice cream.

I had just spent the day telling my mum how well it was going with Anna, and from the tone of Anna's voice, it sounded quite a lot like I was about to be dumped!

My mum, knowing her son's ability to throw himself into situations, had confirmed she was happy to hear how well it was going, but advised me to take it slowly. On the phone call, Anna, who sounded a bit jumpy, asked me if I could just come round to hers instead of us going out with some friends. She had something important to tell me!

As a serial catastrophiser, I, of course, assumed the worst. I was about to get dumped by someone who had realised she couldn't love a man who constantly talked through *Gossip Girl*.

I do vividly remember thinking *this doesn't sound good.* We had gone out for about 18 months and had broken up 5 years previously. Since this was our second attempt after a generous "cooling off" period, I reckoned, I had grounds to fear the worse. Even though it was over a decade ago, I can still remember the conversation and being told that I was almost certainly about to become a dad.

I can't remember much more than I used the time I had until the train departed incredibly wisely. I bought two cans of Fosters and a grab bag of salt and vinegar crisps. I also bought Anna some roses— the flowers, not the chocolates. The journey back to Brighton was spent in a crispy beery daze that would probably be best described as a cocktail of excitement, disbelief and brief moments of fear.

Chapter Takeaways

1. Maintaining a good sense of humour is vital, not just now, but in life. If you remember not to take any emotional outbursts directed at you too personally, you'll be on the right track.
2. Take your partner to her GP appointment.
3. Treat her to an early birthday or Christmas present and buy her some Folic Acid. Nothing says I love you quite like some folic acid.

"When my father didn't have my hand, he had my back."

- Author & Former Priest Linda Poindexter

Chapter 6
Week 6

When Does Our Baby Start Having Features?

Your baby's cheeks, chin and jaw are developing, and who knows, they may be smiling at one of Dad's terrible jokes for the first time!

While conducting research, I noticed that unborn children are often compared to small vegetables. Your baby's crown-to-rump measurement will be between a fifth to a quarter of an inch, which is about the size of a sweet pea.

Your partner is now in the 2nd month of pregnancy, which means only 7 months remain. Your partner is feeling properly pregnant and may describe that as feeling sick, having heartburn, and needing the loo most of the time.

What's The Umbilical Cord?

It's the cord connecting your growing baby with the placenta while he or she is in the uterus. The umbilical cord is clamped and cut at birth; what is left will become your belly button. It looks like a dressing gown cord of sausage meat left out in the rain for a week or two. To raise its PR, remember it's keeping your son or daughter alive, so it deserves a bit of respect.

Who Gets To Cut The Cord?

I imagine the midwife makes a judgement based on the father's complexion and all-around demeanour before offering them the type of scissors you may have seen on *Casualty*.

I had thought about this scenario and how it could play out for me. I knew it would tap into my OCD irrational fears of accidentally hurting people, so I accepted that I would have to ask a midwife the sort of question she'd expect from an anxious child.

Can I Check It's Not Going To Hurt Anyone When I Cut It?

Luckily, my complexion must have passed the test, as I distinctly remember being handed some scissors and asked to cut the cord. In doing so, I experienced a rare win over an obsessive compulsion I'd been trying not to give in to on and off since my teens. What I mean is that this was a rare occasion where I had instinctively trusted myself without needing any external reassurance. Anything medical-related has always potentially been a challenging scenario for me. In that I didn't give in to my anxiety and ask a question about something I already knew the answer to be a fairly big moment. It was one of the first times I can remember a positive emotion being powerful enough to squash any underlying feelings of anxiety.

It was quite a challenge and felt like a thick piece of chorizo sausage. Just to reassure anyone who may have a mind like mine, cutting the umbilical cord doesn't hurt the baby in any way because it doesn't contain any nerves. It won't hurt in the same way that it doesn't hurt you when someone's cutting your hair or you're cutting your own fingernails.

When your partner is 6 weeks pregnant, there will be a prominent bulge where the heart is and another bump at the head end. The embryo is curved and has a tail, so it looks a bit like a tadpole. Or, for any fans of the *Matrix* franchise, a friendlier version of the sentinels that hunt Neo's spaceship in the second film. There are visible arms and legs, best described as small swellings instead of limbs. Some dimples on the head are becoming the ears, and there are two thickenings where the eyes will be.

The developing arms and legs become visible as small swellings (limb buds). The little dimples on the side of the head will become the ears, and there are thickenings where the eyes will be. Your baby is now covered with a layer of skin so thin that it's transparent.

Survival Tip

If you are anxious about being asked to cut the cord, just remember that you may have overcome similar or more significant life challenges. This might sound insane but practising the action itself might not be a completely bonkers idea. Consider it as your first dad test. Suppose you have practised the movement previously, for example, by cutting strips of bacon with kitchen scissors to make yourself a delicious bacon sandwich every Sunday.

In that case, you may find yourself significantly desensitised when the time comes. I've struggled with intrusive thoughts for as long as I can remember. During a CBT course I did with the NHS in 2010, it was suggested that I almost certainly had a form of OCD.

How Can You Support Your Partner, Baby & Yourself In Week 6?

One of the strategies I was taught for me to learn to overcome my compulsion of repeatedly going back to check the front doors or car door is locked was to immerse myself in the anxious feelings. It's not easy the first few times, but like everything, the more you do it, the easier it gets.

These early pregnancy symptoms will affect your relationship. It's often an impact that is viewed as a negative one, but I don't think it has to be considered that way. You can and will learn life lessons from various, often unlikely sources. Wisdom is not exclusively transferred from the old to the young. As your baby is developing thicker skin this week, it may be a good time for you to try and do the same.

I would describe my wife as a northerner. She would argue that Quorn is in the East Midlands. Unless you have webbed feet or gills, everything will be north of Brighton.

Where am I going with this?

Here comes a massive generalisation that will probably be lost on you if you're not from the UK, but she has a "northern" and, therefore, hardcore attitude. She's more of a "getting on with it" and less of a southern softy complainer.

Therefore, being pregnant, if anything, made us closer as a couple. We still had our moments. I remember getting cross in Café Rouge when she refused to eat her meal because she considered melted cheddar a soft cheese!

I also remember her getting cross because I suggested Angus as a potential name. "We're having a baby, not a steakhouse!"

Having a baby must be a potentially terrifying proposition for women but not really as much for men. For her, everything in her life will change. What she eats and drinks is determined by what is best for her baby, and she might feel sick, bloated, and anxious, especially if this is her first pregnancy.

With that in mind, she needs to be cut some slack, and you need to become the calming port in the storm. You may get shouted at for things you don't think are your fault, like not asking a waiter to remove cheese from a burger. You should have realised that regardless of something being described as hard cheese, in the mind of your pregnant partner, it becomes soft cheese when melted, and therefore she doesn't want it.

What we men will never be able to comprehend until after the birth is the anxiety a pregnant woman must feel about the responsibility of growing this little person. I only really have an understanding now that our children are very much outside. I find myself saying, "Be careful," "Watch Out," and "Slow down" more than anything else. As a parent, you will find that you are constantly risk-assessing. The thought of your child coming to any sort of harm is too much to bear, which must be what it feels like for a woman once all the time.

The following 9 months are a test for her but also for you.

You must be the man for her and your baby. If you have a brother or a close friend or work colleague (ideally who is a dad) who, in exchange for beer and crisps, is happy to go for a weekly beer so you can have a moan about all the stuff you might be worried about that might be a sound call. She is busy dealing with the changes to her body and mind, and harsh as it sounds, she won't have any spare time or energy to shoulder your worries. You either need to find a way to self-manage or a close friend who is prepared to listen. Most dads will want to help. We remember what it was like, and you might be surprised how your friendships with any of your dad mates suddenly strengthen.

Chapter Takeaways

1. Tread carefully when suggesting children's names. It's all a bit academic until your child appears, as sometimes they just don't look like a Holly, Peter, or Erasmus. Suggesting an unusual name to try and wind your partner up may backfire as she may really like it. You might end up having a son or daughter that never speaks to you again once they learn that it was you that suggested the name "Zeus Hornblower III!"
2. If you're squeamish about cutting the umbilical cord, discuss it with your partner or start seeing how you feel by cutting some bacon for a weekly bacon sandwich.

3. If you're feeling overwhelmed at becoming a dad but don't want to load more onto your partner, confide in a close friend.

"A good father is one of the most unsung, unpraised, unnoticed, and yet one of the most valuable assets in our society."

- American Evangelist Billy Graham

Chapter 7
Week 7

Will My Partner Be Looking Pregnant Yet?

The beach ball under the jumper stage isn't for a few months, but she will be constantly reminded that she's growing someone whenever Mum feels queasy, bloated or that she'd quite fancy another mango.

"Really? You'd like a 4th mango?"

"Yes, what's your point?"

"Nothing. I'll see if Taj is still open!"

Your partner's womb is now the size of a lemon, 5 times bigger than its original size. From my recent Google search, that's still smaller than an average-sized wombat, so that's something. She's probably tired, her breasts might feel sore and enlarged, and she probably needs to pee more than usual.

In most cases, feelings of nausea and vomiting (morning sickness) start to improve after around week 14 of pregnancy. Your partner may have bleeding or sore gums. Good mouth hygiene and regular dental work is the best way to avoid teeth or gum problems.

The silver lining? Your tired, nauseous partner will no doubt be thrilled to learn she gets her bleeding gums treated for free. All dental care is free during pregnancy and one calendar year after her due date. If she asks her midwife or doctor how to apply for free dental care, they can advise her.

Survival Tip

If your partner's constant trips to the loo are frustrating you, just imagine how it's making her feel. Don't highlight how many times she's been to the loo in the last hour. If you do, don't be surprised if you get a half-eaten mango husk to the side of the head.

Her needing the loo is one of the more common symptoms around this time because the hormone HCG is causing increased blood flow to the pelvic area. This is great news for increased sexual pleasure, but not when you're ten minutes into a theatre production of War Horse. Her kidneys are also becoming more efficient at getting rid of waste products. Her uterus is more prominent, and this is pushing down on her bladder. All of this creates the perfect storm of her needing the loo a lot.

To reduce how often she needs the loo, you can suggest (at your own risk) that she leans forward while she is weeing. This will ensure that her bladder is completely empty. Beware, your well-meaning "pee tip" may encourage another mango husk to the head, so you advise her on this and anything else at your own risk.

How Can You Support Your Partner, Baby & Yourself In Week 7?

You could suggest going for a walk. The light exercise will be as good for your physical and mental health as hers. Going for walks was something we did when Anna was pregnant with all three of our children. I remember it being something that worked particularly with her first pregnancy.

Pamper her. If you can afford to treat her to a massage, then that might earn you serious brownie points not just with her but anyone she tells (mother, work colleagues, a confused-looking postman). If funds are tight, you could pamper her yourself. Give her a massage and watch her favourite film. If she's missing a glass of wine, you could prepare some chocolate-covered strawberries or make avocado brownies which sound rank but must be a healthier alternative.

Chapter Takeaways

1. Your partner is entitled to free dental treatment; offer to drive her to an appointment.
2. Be supportive and start factoring in finding clean toilets on all journeys.
3. If she's tired and heavy, suggest walking together. This is great for physical and mental health and will strengthen your relationship.
4. Give her a neck or foot massage if she's missing a glass of wine at the end of a tough day.

"Nothing ever fits the palm so perfectly, or feels so right, or inspires so much protective instinct as a child's hand."

- Australian Author Gregory David Roberts

Chapter 8
Week 8

When Does Our Baby Become A Baby, Not An Egg?

The magic continues to happen, and at 8 weeks, your baby has decided on a name change from Embryo to Foetus.

Other physical developments will include the legs getting longer; if they have my genetics, that may not be much longer. Your baby is still using its amniotic sac (*first-ever pack lunch*). Luckily, it hasn't noticed that instead of a Babybel, it's been given an off-brand version, Babybill. The placenta is still forming the necessary structures to attach itself to the womb wall.

Your partner's womb is still just the size of a lemon but don't worry, that's still plenty big enough to ensure she's spending the lion's share of her day on the loo, on the way to the loo, coming back from a loo or worrying about when she will next need the loo.

Survival Tip

Regardless of how hysterical it may be if your pregnant girlfriend walks out of a Starbucks toilet with her dress tucked into her pants. It might not be something she's happy for you to mention in a social media post, or book!

How Can You Support Your Partner, Baby & Yourself In Week 8?

At 8 weeks, your partner is feeling tired, may have tender boobs, and anxiety about how she's going to push something the size of a pineapple through the size of an orange. Maybe use any of the "nervous energy" you may also have about becoming a parent to give nightly back and neck massages while telling her how awesome she is.

At 8 weeks, your partner will probably have missed her second period but may still experience some bleeding from her vagina.

What Should My Partner Do If She's Worried About Any Bleeding?

It's always a good idea for her to mention any bleeding during pregnancy to her GP or her midwife. This is way more important if it continues or is accompanied by stomach pain.

If this happens, just calmly try to reassure her. Don't start rushing around trying to diagnose things you're not medically trained to comment on. You'll have times during your partner's 9-month pregnancy when you'll have to put your shared concerns about your partner's welfare and the welfare of your unborn child in a strong box.

Look at it as training for when your daughter rolls off a changing table during the 0.22 seconds it took you to bend down and pick up a swimming nappy; I still have nightmares about that decades on. Your partner is on person growing duty, but you're also having to come to terms with the idea of being a brand-new person. Try to reframe it as you're becoming something quite extraordinary because that's what being a dad is. I'm genuinely excited for you.

You will have moments where you're scared and unsure, but that's a parent's life. My advice is only to comment on what you know and understand. Not only will it really annoy midwives to have a Mr Know-It-All medical man giving his five pence worth, but it won't help calm a panicking partner.

Always take your partner's concerns seriously, even if you can see that the white stuff in your baby's bottom is definitely Sudocrem and not worms. I found that often saying nothing and just listening was the best thing I could do. The female body and what it is during pregnancy are mind-bogglingly intelligent. Your partner will know what to do.

If you must drive her to A & E at 2am because she can't feel the baby kick, try and view it as an adventure you're on together. Look at it as something you're getting to do, not something you have to do. This is your training. You will have lots of these rescue missions to accept and complete when your kids are here. I'm sure it's the stuff that turns an ordinary life into an extraordinary one.

Miscarriage

A miscarriage is the most common loss of life, happening in 1 in 4 pregnancies. Miscarriages at any stage are hugely distressing for both parents, especially Mum.

The leading causes of miscarriage are thought to be the following:

- Genetically there can be problems when the baby doesn't develop right from the very beginning of procreation and, sadly, can't survive. According to recent statistics, this accounts for more than half of all early miscarriages.

- Women with very irregular periods can find it harder to get pregnant, and when they do, they can be more likely to miscarry.
- Blood-clotting issues. If there are problems in the blood vessels supplying the placenta, this can lead to miscarriage and is even more true if the blood clots more than it should.
- Some minor infections, like a common cough or cold, will not be harmful. If the mother was to get a very high fever or a disease like German measles, this could potentially cause a miscarriage.
- Anatomical problems. There are three leading anatomical causes of miscarriage:
- If the cervix (*the bottom of the uterus*) is weak, it may open as the uterus becomes heavier in later pregnancy, which could cause a miscarriage.
- If the uterus has an irregular shape, there may not be enough room for the baby to grow.
- Large fibroids (*harmless growths in the uterus*) may cause miscarriage in later pregnancy.

This info is taken from the miscarriage association. For further information, please visit their website info@miscarriageassociation.org.uk or call their helpline at 01924 200799.

How Could I Comfort & Support My Partner If She Has A Miscarriage?

I pray this doesn't happen to you and your partner. Life can be ruthless and that's why I've included the information above. If it does happen, you have the option to talk to people who are professionally trained to offer the best support. I would definitely do this, even if it's the last thing either of you feels like doing. Here's how I would try and support anyone who is grieving:

- Take your cue from them. If they want to talk, listen more, and talk less.
- If they don't want to talk, make it clear (once, not every 10 minutes) that you're here for them if that ever changes and they do want to talk.
- Be kind and loving.
- Don't say that you know how they feel. Even if you're a woman who has also experienced a miscarriage, everyone's experience is different, so I would avoid saying it at all.
- Cut them some slack and take on more of the shared workload. The cooking and general housework, etc.
- When you do, do it without being asked or needing any congratulations for having done so.

This is probably one for you more than for your partner and, therefore, may offer little to no comfort. I just know it helped me when my dad (to whom this book is dedicated) died in 2020.

Life is short, sometimes cut very short, and actioning these suggestions is much easier said than done. I tried to focus on being grateful that something good had happened rather than focusing on being sad that it had ended. I'm also trying to live my life in a way that honours him. A way that he might be proud of. This was the kick up the arse I needed to remind myself that instead of there being things I must do, there are things I get to do.

Life is a gift, and hopefully, the sadness we will inevitably have to face only helps to highlight how lucky we are to experience it in the first place. That's my two-pence worth anyway.

Chapter Takeaways

1. Your baby is now referred to as a foetus, not an embryo.
2. If your partner has any bleeding and is concerned about it, encourage her to contact her doctor or midwife ASAP. Alternatively, she could seek advice from the NHS 111 helpline.
3. Don't give advice on medical issues you don't know much or anything about.

4. If following your trip to A and E turns out to be a false alarm, be relieved. Focus on being thankful that everyone is okay and not grumpy because you're now a bit tired.

"A good father can smile when there is little to smile about."

\- Anonymous

Chapter 9
Week 9

What's Going An At This Stage?

During the 9-week pregnancy, your baby's little face is slowly forming. The eyes are more significant and will start to contain some colour in them. He or she will also now have a mouth and a tongue with tiny taste buds.

The hands and feet are developing. They haven't separated yet, but they will have ridges that identify where the fingers and toes will be. Your baby's major internal organs, the heart, brain, lungs, and kidneys, continue to develop and grow. Regarding your baby's head-to-rump size, he or she is now approximately 2.2cm, about the length of my wedding band.

At 9 weeks, your partner may find that her breasts have grown, and she might need to invest in a more supportive bra. She may also notice that, as well as bigger breasts, she has more powerful and extreme emotions. The hormonal changes taking place in her body can make her feel very happy one minute and very sad the next.

Survival Tip

Even if you only have the best intentions, I wouldn't suggest saying this to your pregnant partner when she's dealing with a pregnancy-related ailment.

"Yeah, I know just how you feel!"

If she's worried about the pregnancy, she can and should seek professional support from her midwife or GP. This would also be the time for her to start confiding in her friends and relations who are already mums. In that they have been there and done that, they may be able to offer her some practical ideas to help.

If her anxiety is getting to a point where it's negatively affecting her everyday life, I would advise her to talk to a midwife. A midwife can either offer solutions herself or refer her to another medical professional.

How Can You Support Your Partner, Baby & Yourself In Week 9?

Your partner's energy is, rightly so, focused mostly on looking after herself and your unborn baby. Being pregnant and unable to do some things she used to, like unwinding with a glass of wine at the end of the day, might make her tired and scratchy. Remember that we tend to give the toughest treatment to the ones we love the most.

It's not easy to do, but if you can try and reframe this as more evidence of the faith she has in your ability, it will help you both. Your sex life might understandably be taking an extended leave of absence. This can, of course, add pressure to your relationship.

Sex is universally accepted as a fundamental component of a healthy adult relationship. I would argue that men consider sex more of a need than a want. I have often heard other men say that they find sex their primary and, for obvious reasons, "preferred" way to connect with their partner. I imagine any women reading this may consider that quite convenient!

I've also heard that a man falls in love through his eyes and a woman falls in love through her ears. That said, it's not always the case that a woman doesn't want sex during pregnancy. You might find that, in the second and third trimesters, it feels a bit strange to have sex with a heavily pregnant partner. Not from a lack of desire but more that you don't want to hurt her or freak out your unborn child.

Sexual frustration is often present, and you may need to find another way to take the situation in hand (excuse the pun) if you don't want it to add pressure to this already pressurised state. Try putting yourself in her shoes. For starters, her shoes might not fit or be painful as her feet can swell when pregnant.

How sexy would you feel if you were constantly aware that there was a person growing inside you? How "up for it" would you feel if you were primarily responsible for the safe birth of your child? For a dad, it's only once your child is mobile and constantly banging its head on every sharp corner in your home that we understand the worry. Or when your baby is finally quiet, and you're checking they're breathing every five minutes. Only then can we grasp the pressure a woman may be trying to deal with from day one.

The only way for us men to really understand would be if it was biologically possible to do a gestational job-share. The man and woman sharing the 9 months-growing project. Men did the first trimester, women did the second, and we could rock, paper, scissors for the third? If that was possible, I think that would help us men find a way to quieten our physical needs.

If you see this as a test of resilience and an opportunity to show your partner she made the right choice, that's a good outcome. Either that or start taking icy cold showers on a daily basis. Find a friend to confide in if you can't talk to your partner about relationship worries. Ideally, a friend who has already successfully navigated himself through a pregnancy.

What doesn't kill you makes you stronger; the adage is true. Your relationship will be all the stronger when you get through this. Yes, it will be a challenge, but if you can work through the tough times, it will be a challenge you can enjoy overcoming together.

The glasses of wine I have with my wife when we've both had to work together to literally wrestle our three children into bed were always the most satisfying because they felt so genuinely earnt. You will struggle, but if you can keep working, keep choosing to be kind before being right and keep your sense of humour, you will find yourself on the other side together as a happy and stable family.

Chapter Takeaways

1. The hormonal changes in her body may have made her breasts significantly bigger. You might need to treat her to a supportive bra to reduce pain in her lower back. There will already be more stress on

her back from the weight of her baby bump. For help with this, these guys seem to know what they are on about: www.bravissimo.com

2. This is easier said than done, but if your partner "understandably" isn't interested in sex while pregnant and it's worrying you, talk to her. I imagine that she's just more focused on the concept of growing and pushing out a baby. That said, checking that there isn't a bigger problem and finding other ways to connect intimately shows that you are committed to strengthening your relationship. I think it's natural for anyone to feel insecure if someone who recently wanted to have sex with them suddenly seems not to.
3. The best way to get through this is with some, ideally, calm and non-confrontational communication. People can get defensive or emotional is they feel they are being confronted on sensitive topics like sex or money.
4. Confide in a close friend. Talking to other like-minded dads who have been through the process really helps. You may realise that what you're going through is very typical.

"Being a good dad starts with presence, not presents."

- Anonymous

Chapter 10
Week 10

What Vaccinations Might My Partner Be Advised To Have?

As part of her maternity care, she will be offered screening to determine the baby's chance of having Down's syndrome, Edward's syndrome and Patau's syndrome.

Pregnant women and their babies are at higher risk from flu (influenza) and whooping cough (pertussis). She will be advised to have the flu and whooping cough vaccination to protect herself and her baby.

How Big Is The Baby Now?

Regarding the head-to-rump measurement, at this stage, your baby will be approx. 4cm. To stay consistent with the comparisons to small food items, that's about the length of an almond. Your baby's development is progressing nicely. He or she now has ears developing on the side of the head and ear canals forming inside the skull. He or she may be listening and wondering what the fascination with creating midlife crisis raps while showering is all about.

Straight out of East Sussex,

A crazy muddy funster called Jim Dog!

Twice a week, jiu-jitsu, then maintain a blog!

Got my fingers crossed that a book takes off?

I'm frustrated when a latte is mostly froth!

I'm British, so don't queue-jump me!

If you do, I'll be seething internally!

When Do We Get The First Look At Our Baby's Face?

You won't be able to see your baby's face at the 12-week scan, which is usually the first opportunity to see any image of your baby and hear its heartbeat.

If you could zoom in, you'd be able to see that he or she now have an upper lip and two tiny nostrils. Your baby's jawbones are also developing and will already contain the future milk teeth.

A heart is now formed, and the heartbeat often ends up being a high point of the 12-week scan. It's the evidence that confirms the grainy, black, and white image you're looking at is your baby.

His or her heart is beating at approx. 180 beats a minute. To put this into perspective, that's about 2 to 3 times faster than your adult heartbeat but not quite as fast as a humming-bird's, which is 1,260 beats per minute. Babies' hearts beat at the same speed as a rabbit or an anesthetised rhesus monkey, according to the MSD Veterinary manual. This heart rate is what's powering the small and jerky movements you might be able to pick out at your 12-week ultrasound scan.

Survival Tip

When giving your partner advice on the optimum dietary requirements during pregnancy, I would advise offering this advice via text message, preferably from a different room or, even better, time zone!

How Can You Support Your Partner, Baby & Yourself In Week 10?

Your partner may be getting sick and tired of feeling sick. The only advice I can offer is to encourage her to rest as much as possible. If this means you have to become the Mrs Doubtfire of the house, then so be it. When it comes to cooking, avoid any especially strongly smelling food, as this can be a significant trigger.

Other smells, like cigarette smoke, may also make her feel sick. Encouraging your partner, while making sure your titanium helmet is strapped on, to drink little and often and have more frequent but smaller meals throughout the day can help reduce feelings of sickness.

My advice is to take the lead in managing the house, shopping, etc. I don't say this to blow my trumpet or shine a light on how awesomely progressive I am, but there really isn't a woman's or man's work. There's just work, especially when it comes to raising a family!

If you live together, your partner becoming pregnant may be your first experience of having to take the reins regarding the housework. This may feel strange to begin with, but I assure you there is an unparalleled satisfaction that can come from keeping a house clean, feeding, and caring for those you love. I worked in the French Alps as a chalet host for a winter season, and it was one of the happiest times of my life.

Like other things I mentioned, if you can start to view this as something you "get to" not "have to" do for your family, that can improve your perspective. The NHS website is one I'm using as a reference point for this book. It's a sad indicator that in every chapter on "What to Expect During Pregnancy," there is a reference to domestic violence and how to seek support from it.

There is never a scenario where domestic violence is acceptable.

Less so during any of my wife's pregnancies, but I've had times as a dad where the kids have managed to push me to the point where I've had to pull my own emergency chute. The best advice I can offer when you feel like you are about to erupt is to remove yourself from the house. Obviously, only do this if it's safe to do so and then take a slow, calming walk around the block.

If you're the only adult in the house, then realistically, you can only remove yourself from the room and the child/children who may be making you feel close to tears. There have been moments in the past when I've had to do this. When I did, I remained close enough to make sure the kids were safe but further away to give myself a moment of calm.

I found that slowly counting ten deep breaths, a count of two on the inhale and four on the exhale really calmed me down. Doing this before you end up saying or do something you regret is a strong call. If you can make and action this before shouting and scaring your family, you will have won that parenting battle.

My Partner Doesn't Like Hospitals. Does She Have To Give Birth In One?

I imagine the men and women who have lashed out in anger probably regret that one decision beyond any other. I would like to think it would be possible to be forgiven and forgive someone for pretty much anything. I'm not sure violence of any kind is something that could ever be forgiven, especially in your home.

Some people are terrified of hospitals. People who suffer extreme fear of hospitals are said to have Nosocomephobia. Apparently, it's one of the more common phobias. I suppose the fear of going into one might mean you won't be coming out. There are, as I see it, three options when it comes to where you can give birth.

1. At home
2. A midwife-led unit (birth centre)
3. A hospital.

The decision will depend on where you live and any health problems or needs your partner has.

My wife was adamant about giving birth in the hospital, and I agreed. We are blessed in the UK to have one of if not the best healthcare services in the world. I have never been anything other than hugely impressed and grateful for my experiences in NHS hospitals. Why wouldn't you want the best medical attention, resources and support for your partner and baby?

Here are some reasons why I think NHS staff are epic and should all be given massive pay raises or at least enough so they don't have to worry about money and can just focus on being the angels that live amongst us:

- The midwife who observed my wife placing both hands on a Citroen Saxo before letting out a noise I would best describe as bovine. To a passer-by, what may have looked like a scene from a "World's Strongest Pregnant Lady Tournament" was just another big contraction. We later learnt the midwife was on her way home but obviously recognised something in my wife's groan that justified her immediate attention. *"You're well on the way. I'm going to walk you up."*
- The doctor who assured me that I didn't need to mop the floor. I had fainted and wet myself in front of a room full of medical staff and a girl I was trying to impress. She had come off her mountain bike and having some stitches put in her chin. It wasn't my proudest moment.
- The midwife for my wife's last labour. She demonstrated a masterclass in how to manage pregnant ladies who keep saying sorry, and sorry for saying sorry. She also worked her midwifery

ninja mind tricks on me. A man who clearly had a major fear of sharps boxes and medical bins.

- The midwife who held a hand fan over my head during my wife's second labour. True to form, I had pulled a massive whitey and was on all fours trying not to pass out like a big wally.
- The anaesthetist who got me an extra blanket and reassured me that regardless of age, it's normal for people to shake with fear if they have never had surgery before.

You might view your kitchen floor differently once you've watched your partner give birth on it. Or that orangery may give off medical vibes if it once housed a *Paw Patrol* paddling pool. That body of water that had included every possible body fluid, plus some you didn't know existed.

Everyone should experience the quintessentially British tradition that seems to come as standard when giving birth in an NHS hospital. It's surreal. You're both in a room that looks like a closing scene from a Quentin Tarantino film, and a midwife suddenly wheels in celebratory tea and toast for two. Those three cups of tea I had with my wife following the birth of each of our children, as we both looked out of the 13th-floor window as a new day crept lazily off the eastern arm of the Brighton Marina, will always be the best three cups I ever had.

Chapter Takeaways

1. Your baby is about the same size as an almond at this stage.
2. Your partner may feel very tired. Instead of getting frustrated at your increased housework, let it empower you. Use this as an opportunity to learn some domestic skills. Look after your partner, grab your marigolds, and get to work.
3. There are three options for where you can give birth. In a hospital, a midwife-led unit or at home. Spend time talking to other people who have been through this experience to get differing perspectives. Labour can be messy and, at times, stressful. I would always want medical people with access to all the best kit to support my wife and baby. I'm also not sure if I'd ever be able to relax in our kitchen, if it ended up looking the way all three of our maternity rooms did!

"One thing that prevents a man from being a good father is he hasn't completed being a boy."

- American Inspirational Speaker Iyanla Vanzant

Chapter 11
Week 11

How To React When She Has A Headache

It depends on the degree of the headache, as they can be everyday things during pregnancy. This is due to the constant changes going on in her body. Headaches are expected in early pregnancy and, like the feelings of morning sickness, tend to become less of an issue as her pregnancy goes on. It's important to note that unpleasant as they are, they won't harm your baby.

That said, if the headaches are persistent and causing vision problems, then you should call your midwife, doctor or hospital. A severe headache, vision problems and sudden swelling on your hands, feet, face or stomach could be a sign of pre-eclampsia.

This serious pregnancy condition can be hazardous for your partner and baby if it's not monitored and treated.

Survival Tip

Remarkable as it is a resource to find videos of cats falling off Christmas trees, the internet can be dangerous if it's in the hands of an anxious pregnant lady with a penchant for self-diagnosis.

If your partner is concerned about an ailment, the best advice I can give is this:

- Don't make fun of them or get cross.
- Listen to her but only comment on what you're qualified to.
- Advise her to call the NHS non-emergency number 111. They will always be able to gather the correct information. If she needs to escalate the situation, then ring 999 or visit the local A & E department asap.

How Can You Support Your Partner, Baby & Yourself In Week 11?

The short answer is lots.

The placenta that provides your baby with its oxygen and nutrients is developing rapidly and will be fully formed at about 12 weeks. The bones of the face are created, and the eyelids are closed and won't open for a few months. Anyone with teenage children can probably relate to this.

The ears continue to develop on the baby's head and now look more like ears than thickening areas of skin. Your baby's head is still big compared to the rest of its body and, at 11 weeks, can make up one-third of its length. That said, in this bizarre two-horse head vs body race, the body is starting to catch up and straighten out.

If you could hold your baby in the palm of your hand, its head-to-rump length would be about 1.6 inches.

Maternity Leave

Your partner must inform her employer about the pregnancy at least 15 weeks before the due date. If this is 40 weeks, she must inform the boss at week 25. Many women tell their employer after the 12-week scan, about the same time work colleagues may have stopped offering the biscuits.

Your boss will need to provide her all the information about paid maternity leave. She is legally entitled to paid time off for all her antenatal care. This includes her appointments with her midwife.

Even though you are entitled to it, it might be a good idea to be as helpful as possible to your employer. Your paid maternity leave is something you're legally entitled to. It might help your partner to be mindful that her absence will probably put added pressure on her colleagues.

Some people might say that her being pregnant will increase your boss's and team's workload. Your employer can ask you for proof of appointments, so offering to provide these before they ask might go down well. As your baby's father, you are entitled to attend two antenatal appointments, for example (the 12 and 20-week scan), but they are unpaid.

Does My Partner Being Pregnant Change What Work They Can Ask Her To Do?

The simple answer is no. It's essential to be aware that, sadly, pregnant employees have been and, I imagine, will continue to be subject to unfair treatment, dismissal, or discrimination. Your partner's contracted terms and conditions cannot be changed without her agreement.

Your employer will legally have to provide an up-to-date workplace risk assessment. With that in mind, once she has informed them that she's pregnant, they will have to make sure your workplace is safe for her to work in. If, for whatever reason, they deem that it is not safe, it's their responsibility to make the necessary changes. If they can't, they will have to provide her with alternative work for the same pay. They would also need to review any potential health and safety risks to your partner during her pregnancy.

Is There Danger My Partner Will Be Mistreated Once They Learn She's Pregnant?

On the contrary, once your employer learns that your partner's pregnant, she is more protected against unfavourable treatment. Your boss has to record any pregnancy-related sickness separately so that it can't be used against her in disciplinary, redundancy or dismissal decisions.

It's good practice to email your boss as opposed to telling them in the lift or while you're eating your lunch for the simple reasons that:

- Your partner will then have a paper trail if, for any reason, she feels she has been discriminated against.
- It's a professional way to behave, which I imagine your boss will appreciate. As well as being the correct way to behave, it may make their work-life balance slightly more manageable.
- The vital information to include is the date she would ideally like to start her leave and maternity pay.
- She needs to have provided this information by the end of the 15th week before her 40-week due date.

As much as you want your mate to have the exclusive, it might not go down well if your boss hears about this on the grapevine.

Your being pregnant may require work-related decisions that have to be managed before it becomes common knowledge.

What Should My Partner Do If Her Boss Reacts Negatively To Her Pregnancy?

As disappointing as this is, I imagine it happens frequently. It's a fact of life that most people will be thinking about how your change affects them first. If your boss handles it poorly, try not to get upset and remind yourself of the following.

- You are entitled to a career and a family, and you shouldn't be made to feel bad about wanting both.
- How they react says nothing about you but everything about them.
- Once your partner is someone's mum, she might find that the distant memory of a work-related issue that seemed a big deal at the time no longer is.
- There is lots of practical and pragmatic advice online to help you deal appropriately with any adverse treatment you may receive due to your pregnancy.

Without wanting to overload your employer with information, it might be helpful to include the following information in her "I'm pregnant!" email. Not only will this show that you know what you're entitled to, but you're keen to be as helpful as possible.

- Your career goals and aspirations: Your boss may have to go to his boss and discuss your role beyond your maternity leave. Knowing what you want, long term, before you get to that point can only help.
- The organisation's maternity and shared leave policies. It will come across as professional and show you are aware of your legal rights.
- Make sure you know your annual leave and suggest dates for how and when you might want to use it.
- Detail what, if any, options you would be prepared to discuss regarding flexible working or job shares etc.
- Make sure you mention the significant dates that can't be negotiated reasonably early in the email. For example 12-week scan, 20-week scan, all midwife appointments

Chapter Takeaways

1. If your partner is having regular headaches, take it seriously and don't self-diagnose. A call to her midwife or NHS 111 will help her decide if she needs medical support.
2. Legally, your partner doesn't have to let her

employer know she's pregnant until week 25 but giving as much notice as possible is sensible. I would notify them via email, detailing what dates you need off and your work aspirations beyond giving birth.

3. Tell your boss before your workmates. If your boss hears the news from Dave in accounts, it won't go down well.

"The guys who fear becoming fathers don't understand that fathering is not something perfect men do, but something that perfects the men."

- "Ask Dr Frank Pittman" American Psychiatrist

Chapter 12
Week 12

What Happens At The 12-Week Scan?

The sheer fact that our first 12 weeks still sticks in my mind about a decade on must mean it had a profound effect on me.

At the 12-week stage, your foetus is now fully formed. All its muscles, bones, and limbs are in place, including the organs that determine his or her gender. This is also the first time in the pregnancy where the two worlds of what is happening in there and out there collide.

I imagine other countries provide similar services for pregnant women. We're fortunate in the UK because ultrasound scans provided are free. The only expense is the £5 it costs you if you want to buy a picture of your scan.

This image will then live on your fridge door until it's replaced in a few years by your child's first painting. The smart money says that's a print of their hand, foot, or something using half a potato.

The official term for this scan is the dating *scan*, and it's to:

1. See how far along your partner is in her pregnancy and check your baby's development.
2. It can also be part of a screening test for Down's syndrome.
3. It might be a penny-drop moment that your lives are about to change dramatically.
4. The 12-week scan is a good opportunity for you to ask any questions you may have. If you listen carefully, you might find that many questions you have will be answered as the scan unfolds.

This scan may create some positive core memories for you both. It did for me. You're going to be someone's dad, which is the pinnacle of a man's achievements. The world accepts you if you're a man who is trying his best to be a good father.

You can have an average career, and little to no social status but still be looked upon with respect if you're a man doing his best for his family. Need an example, just look at Homer Simpson. He's a character that effectively encapsulates all men's negative characteristics. If you had no prior knowledge of *The Simpsons* and watched an episode, I would imagine most people would view him as more of a hero than a villain. Even though his attempts at pretty much any endeavour are often woefully short of the mark, he's clearly doing his best for his family.

It is helpful for your partner, not you, to have a full bladder for the scan. On current form, this won't be a problem for your partner. A full bladder can make the ultrasound image clearer. The ultrasound usually takes 20 to 30 minutes and can be emotional. Your partner may have many questions, some of which result from nerves. Like me, you may also feel nervous and see lots of opportunities to make witty comments. I advise keeping your Alan Partridge and Borat impressions under lock and key.

The other thing that will make this pregnancy feel more real is your now green light to tell family and friends your news. Like me, you may feel it's necessary to also tell the man in the corner shop, the postman and anyone else you bump into during the next 6 months. I would think carefully about who you tell and in what order. Not everyone will potentially be as thrilled at your news as you are. My advice is to tell your boss and inner circle first. A nice thing to do which, in retrospect, is something I wish I had done, is construct an email so you can tell all your important people and your boss simultaneously. The benefit of this is that you may end up with some lovely emails you can refer to when it's 3am, and you're waiting for your newborn to finally go to sleep.

Survival Tip

If your partner wants a grainy black-and-white image of the scan, don't question it; just buy her one. From memory, they are about £5.

Chapter Takeaways

1. The "actual" time your partner is being scanned is only about 20-30 mins. But, I wouldn't try and shoehorn the first time you see your child into your half-hour lunch break. You may need help finding a parking space or end up having to wait an hour to be seen.
2. Book this day off work and make it an event.
3. If, like me, you can be a wally when you're nervous, try and keep the jokes to a minimum. This is a very big day for you both, especially your partner. Instead of treating the scan lady to another of your hysterical Borat impressions, try to listen and take it all in "*Thank you, please, I like you!*" I recommend sharing your news in an email. As well as close friends and family, this would be an excellent way to let your employer know.

"The older I get, the smarter my father seems to get."

- American Journalist Tim Russert

Chapter 13
Week 13

Why Can Being Pregnant Make You Constipated?

Not everyone gets constipated during pregnancy, but it is one of the more common ailments. Your partner may find that she gets stomach pain or cramps, which are usually nothing to worry about. They're most likely due to wind, your partner's ligaments growing or constipation as her womb gets bigger. She needs to see her midwife or doctor if the stomach pain doesn't go away, becomes severe, or includes some bleeding. In extreme cases, she should call 999 straight away.

Survival Tip

Before my job as a seafront officer, I worried about calling 999. I was concerned that my call would delay someone who may need emergency help more than I did. Having worked alongside the emergency services at work since 2014, I've probably called 999 a few hundred times. These will have been for all sorts of incidents, ranging from lost children to literal life-and-death situations.

If you need an ambulance, you can help them locate you by providing them with your postcode and your "what3words" reference. If you need to familiarise yourself with "what three words," here is how they describe themselves on the website.

https://what3words.com/about

"Street addresses need to be more accurate to specify precise locations, such as building entrances and they also don't exist for parks and many rural areas. This makes it hard to find places and prevents people from describing where help is needed in an emergency."

If the time allows and you remember, always ask the call handler for the (job number) or (incident reference number) so that if you call them back to stand it down, they can find you on the system.

All calls are recorded and can be traced, and if found guilty of a hoax call, you could go to prison for up to 6 months and receive a £5,000 fine.

Chapter Takeaways

1. Stomach cramps are a common ailment during pregnancy. In most cases, it's due to wind, your partner's ligaments growing as her womb gets bigger or constipation.
2. If the stomach pain doesn't go away, becomes severe, or includes bleeding, you need to see your midwife or doctor. In extreme cases, you should call 999 straight away.
3. If you have to call 999, speak calmly and clearly, and only give the information the call handler specifically asks you for. Then give the call handler the postcode for wherever you are.
4. Find out what the "what 3 words" are for your house, her house, places of work etc.
5. Trust your gut when it comes to hers. If you think your partner's stomach pains are beyond a call to your midwife or the NHS 111 number, then call 999.

Take an incident reference number. If the situation fixes itself before an ambulance arrives. You can call 999 again and support some overworked/underpaid emergency workers and stand the case down.

"I cannot think of any need in childhood as strong as the need for a father's protection."

- Austrian Neurologist Sigmund Freud

Chapter 14
Week 14

My Partner Still Wants Sex, Will It Damage The Baby?

It's not always the man who's most keen for sex, and your partner may experience an increased sex drive during pregnancy. This is probably a result of pregnancy hormones or increased blood flow to the pelvic area. It's also understandable if she doesn't, as feeling sick, constipated, flatulent or tired aren't exactly the ideal aphrodisiacs. According to the NHS website, it's totally safe to have sex during pregnancy unless, for some reason, your doctor or midwife has previously advised you not to.

A common concern for dads is that having sex at any stage of pregnancy could hurt or unsettle the baby. Having just watched a video on the NHS website, this is apparently a very common concern from dads. Your penis or a penetrative sex toy will not penetrate beyond your partner's vagina, and the baby can't tell what's going on. There is no "normal" regarding what either of you does or doesn't want regarding sex, and it will differ entirely from couple to couple. The best advice I can give on this topic is to communicate your wants and needs to each other. There are numerous ways to remain intimate during pregnancy beyond penetrative sex if neither of you are keen.

Can Orgasms Or Sex Itself Start Labour Off?

Much later in pregnancy, around or after your due date, an orgasm or penetrative sex itself can set off mild contractions. Your partner would feel her womb's muscles harden, which can be uncomfortable. These contractions are referred to as Braxton Hicks contractions and aren't anything to worry about. Your doctor or midwife may actually advise you to try sex if you are past your due date as a way to get things moving. This may be the last thing either of you wants, but that's the advice you may receive.

If your partner has had any heavy bleeding in her pregnancy due to a low placenta or a blood collection, your medical professional may advise abstaining from sex.

They may also advise against you having sex if:

- There are any issues with the entrance to your partner's womb. Sex, in this instance, could encourage early labour or miscarriage.
- If your partner has been told she is having twins.
- Your partner has previously had early labours before, and she is now in the later stages of her pregnancy.
- If you or your pregnant partner are having sex with other people. If this is the case, it's imperative to use a barrier form of contraception, for example, a condom, to protect both you and, more importantly, your baby from contracting an STD. (*sexually transmitted disease*)
- If your partner's waters have broken, this could increase the chances of infection.

Although we've established that sex for most couples is safe, it might not always be that easy. You might need to change your preferred positions because of the beach ball-sized bump that's in the way. You may also need to alter your sexual default settings because your partner's breasts feel sore or very sensitive. Having sex when your partner is on top of you may be uncomfortable for her as you may feel too deep.

Survival Tip

As previously mentioned, the ability to develop a thicker skin and navigate an ever-changing mood is a game changer. With that in mind, don't be offended if she laughs off your suggestion that you don't want to have sex with her on top because it might feel too big. If it makes you feel better, my wife, who was busy making the kids' pack lunches when I just read this out to her, had a little chuckle to herself before kissing me on the cheek and leaving the room!

This simple rule may help. If it doesn't feel comfortable for either of you for whatever reason, stop and find a comfortable position for *both* of you.

- Lying on your sides facing each other.
- You being on top in the missionary position.
- You're behind while your partner is on her hands and knees. Your partner uses pillows to make it more comfortable.

Chapter Takeaways

1. Due to hormonal changes or an increased blood flow to her pelvic area, your partner may want to have sex
2. Sex is fine unless, for any reason, your midwife or doctor has advised abstaining from it.

3. Sex at this stage of pregnancy won't damage or scare the baby. The best rule to go by is to find a position that you *both* feel most comfortable with.

"Every father should remember one day his son will follow his example, not his advice."

- American Inventor & Engineer Charles Kettering

Chapter 15
Week 15

Is It Normal For My Partner To Put On Weight During Pregnancy And If So, How Much?

When your partner is pregnant, she may understandably be feeling hungrier. Although I imagine you will have heard the idea that she needs to eat for two, that's a myth. Instead, she would be advised to focus more on the nutritional content of food rather than the amount. The NHS website advises that your partner is likely to gain 10 to 12kg during her pregnancy: that's 1.5 to 1.8 stone.

Gaining too much weight or not gaining enough can create health problems for your partner, baby or both. Your midwife or GP will no doubt be able to offer her more advice and support on this topic.

Survival Tip

Even if you meant it as loving or supportive advice, the topic of your partner's weight will always be the main event in Relationship Olympics. If she ever asks you if you think she's getting fat, you must follow these steps to avoid a one-way ticket to the spare room.

1. Don't look at her or even in her general direction.
2. Reply with a loud and firm "*No*" within 1 second or less of the question.

In all seriousness, your partner's pregnant size and weight may create increased or new feelings of insecurity. The best way to support her is to continue complimenting her and showing her affection. But not too much.

What's Happening For Our Baby At This 15-Week Stage?

At this stage of pregnancy, your baby will start to hear noises around it. These noises will include your partner's digestive system gurgling, muted noises from the outside world, the sounds of your partner's voice and her heartbeat. Your baby's eyes may also begin to sense light. The eyes are still closed but may sense a bright light from outside your partner's tummy.

All the changes happening to your partner's body during pregnancy will make it normal for her to experience more vaginal discharge. She will instinctively know what looks and feels normal. Vaginal discharge is usually clear or milky white and shouldn't smell bad. If it does smell bad or it's painful for her to urinate, she needs to contact her midwife ASAP, as this could indicate she has an infection.

Chapter Takeaways

1. Needing to eat for two is a myth; instead, focus on the nutritional value of her food.
2. Your partner will feel hungry, and it's normal for her to put on 10-12kg during pregnancy.
3. Your partner may feel insecure about her weight and looks during pregnancy. Help to support her by showing lots of affection.
4. The only time your partner needs to worry about vaginal discharge is if it smells, she's sore or itchy or if it's painful when she wees. If she has any of these symptoms, she needs to contact her GP or midwife asap as she may have an infection.

"I was selfish before. Everyone is. But when you have kids, they become your main priority."

First Time Dad

- English Football Legend David Beckham

Chapter 16
Week 16

Does My Partner Have To Pay For Prescriptions?

She might have to work hard to see this as a perk, but your partner is entitled to free prescriptions and dental care during pregnancy and 1 year after the birth. Having to pay for haemorrhoid cream could feel like a secondary insult, so hopefully it's something. Your partner will need to fill in a MATB1 form, which she can get from her midwife. (*Relevant only to the UK.*)

Survival Tip

To hopefully take the edge off her pregnancy-related ailments slightly by collecting her free prescriptions, it may be blindingly obvious to whoever is serving you that the medicine isn't for you, but it's probably not a bad idea to take her completed MATB1 form with you. For even more brownie points, I have found that a large bar of Dairy Milk chocolate accompanies free prescriptions well. This act of kindness won't necessarily help with how she views her constipation or backache, but it may improve how she views you and your relationship.

How Can You Support Your Partner, Baby & Yourself In Week 16?

Why not book yourselves up for free antenatal classes? Your partner has enough to deal with, and finding your local group and getting enrolled, will show support. The classes usually start for couples between the 30th and 32nd week of pregnancy. Antenatal classes are a great place to meet others in the same position, but as mentioned, not for telling jokes about hormones. We both made some good friends, and my wife found both the information and support from the other mums really valuable.

Chapter Takeaways

1. Your baby's facial muscles can now move, but they can't control them. These movements will develop into the start of their facial expressions.
2. Your partner will be advised to have her vaccine for whooping cough. It's recommended that its best

to have this anytime from week 16 to week 32 of pregnancy.

3. Your partner doesn't pay for prescriptions during her pregnancy or the first year after birth. Signing up for antenatal classes can be an excellent way to get information and support from other couples in the same position. Your partner is advised to have a vaccine for whooping cough any time from this week to week 32 of her pregnancy.

"The only way I can describe fatherhood is at the end of How the Grinch Stole Christmas; you know how his heart grows like five times? Everything is full; it's just full all the time."

- American Actor Matt Damon

Chapter 17
Week 17

What's The Advice About Drinking Alcohol?

She won't want to hear or be reminded of this but drinking alcohol when pregnant is considered a bad idea.

From all the research I did for this book, the general consensus was that when a woman tries to conceive and becomes pregnant, it's best to stop drinking alcohol altogether. Drinking alcohol increases the chances of miscarriage. It can damage the baby's developing cells and negatively affect how their organs and their brain grow. It can affect how they look, and it can cause them to be born underweight. It can also cause a condition called foetal alcohol spectrum disorder.

This is when a pregnant woman drinks alcohol and has it in her blood, the alcohol is passed on to her unborn baby through the placenta.

The alcohol can stay in your baby's body for a long time because it can't process it effectively.

According to recent statistics, about 3 children in every 100 have FASD. It might not be detected at birth, but it can appear later in life. According to information taken from the NHS website, mothers who drink while pregnant can give birth to:

- Children with learning and behavioural difficulties.
- Children who struggle with balance and movement.
- Children that struggle to effectively manage their emotions and develop social skills.
- Children that can struggle with hyperactivity and maintaining attention.
- Children that can struggle to make friends.
- Children who can struggle to make sense of the world or keep themselves safe.
- Children who have communication issues, such as problems with their speech development.
- Children who are more prone to being singled out and bullied.

- Children who have problems with their joints, muscles and bones.
- Children who have problems with their organs, like their kidneys and heart.

Survival Tip

When your partner gives up drinking alcohol during pregnancy, support her by either not drinking around her or by giving up yourself.

How Can You Support Your Partner, Baby & Yourself In Week 17?

If she makes the commitment to stop drinking alcohol, you could show your support, not just to her, but your baby by doing the same. There will be enough worry about your baby's health without adding one about alcohol consumption damaging his or her development.

If you used to hang out at the pub, it might make sense to pick a hobby where you are not confronted by alcohol. Try to focus on the positives of being teetotal, of which there are many. Here are a few:

- No more hangovers, which can lead to better mental health.
- Increased levels of energy and better quality of sleep.

- Your skin will look better.
- You'll be saving money, and you may even lose some weight.

How Heavy Is Our Baby At This Stage?

He or she is growing and weighs about 150g, about the same weight as a large apple or baseball.

Your baby now has eyelashes. Even though their eyelids are shut, they can move their eyes. They now have their own unique fingerprint, and if you could, you would find that he or she has a firm hand grip.

Chapter Takeaways

1. Drinking *any* alcohol while pregnant isn't a good idea. This is much easier said than done. If you support her by not drinking, you will have set an excellent example of supporting each other and overcoming challenges.

"A father doesn't tell you that he loves you. He shows you."

- Dimitri The Stoneheart

Chapter 18
Week 18

When Is It Possible To Find Out The Baby's Gender?

Your partner will typically be offered two ultrasound scans during her 9-month pregnancy. The first one, as mentioned around week 12, where amongst other things, they will:

- Check your baby is growing as expected
- Find out how many babies there are
- Confirm that the baby is growing inside your partner's womb
- Check your baby for chromosomal anomalies

The foetus isn't developed enough to ascertain a gender at 12 weeks, but this can often be established at a 20-week scan. In our case, only after I'd bought my wife a Mars bar, escorted her down two flights of stairs, and we'd done some star jumps.

Can You Tell Your Child's Gender By The Speed Of Their Heart Rate?

You may hear old wives' tales about how you can establish your child's gender. Here are 7 I found after a quick Google search:

1. If you do or don't have the pregnancy glow. You're having a boy if your complexion is bright and your hair is bushy and bouncy, like a recently conditioned retriever. If you're not, it's a girl, as apparently little girls will steal their mum's good looks.
2. Apparently, excessive morning sickness indicates you're having a girl.
3. If you gain weight as your pregnant partner does, out of sympathy, apparently, you're carrying a girl.
4. If your partner's general mood is best described as a bit moody, it's a girl. If you'd describe her mood as mellow, it's a boy. As a parent of both genders, I can assure you that's the wrong way round, for us anyway.
5. A high baby bump means you're having a girl. A low baby bump means a boy.

6. Tie a ring to a piece of string and hang it over your belly. If it swings in a circular motion, it's a girl; if it moves side to side, it's a boy.
7. And finally, the heart rate test. If your baby's heart rate is over 140 beats per minute, it's a girl. If it's below 140, it's a boy.

This is all lovely but doesn't stop it being considered total bollocks by anyone in the know. When I say, *"in the know,"* I don't mean the odd couple at number 14 that breed stoats.

How Can You Support Your Partner, Baby & Yourself In Week 18?

Your baby may start to visibly move around. In the latter stages of my wife's first pregnancy, I remember seeing what looked like a small heel knock a bag of Maltesers off her stomach. Your baby may respond to loud noises such as music, and this might be another light bulb moment for you. Seeing the rolling or fluttering of your unborn children is remarkable.

Continue to do what you can to support your partner both emotionally and physically. Pure acts of kindness, like scampering through your flat naked to turn off a CD—a compact disc that had been kindly suggested by a friend's yoga teacher but had also been skipping for a good 20 minutes.

"Your uterus will open like a warm, glowing oyster shell. Shimmering with warmth and welcoming your child to the world. To the world...to the world and welcoming your child to the world, an experience without anxiety, cross words, or pain... argh, ya bastard!"

I can assure you there were angry words and pain when I stubbed my toe on a coffee table en route to punch a second-hand CD player. This experience was worsened by my wife, who I could hear snorting and giggling hysterically from the next room. Vulnerable areas responsible for being in this position in the first place flipped around as I tried to establish if I might need an ambulance. The experience may not have awoken my wife's subconscious of untapped mystical shimmering oyster opening skills, but it did make her laugh.

Chapter Takeaways

1. Your partner may be feeling more noticeable fluttering and small kicks. Talking to her bump can increase this and help the bonding process between you and your unborn son or daughter.
2. Remember to move coffee tables back to their original place once your partner has finished doing pregnancy yoga.

First Time Dad

"Dads are most ordinary men turned by love into heroes, adventurers, storytellers and singers of songs."

- Australian Poet Pam Brown

Chapter 19
Week 19

Is Yoga Safe To Do While She's Pregnant?

Labour is called labour for a reason and can go on for days. It's something she will need to prepare for, both physically and mentally. Labour is exercise, and the fitter she is, the easier it will be for her to deal with and adapt to her body's changing shape, weight gain and the exertion of her labour.

Activities like power walking, dancing, yoga and swimming are great for her and not dangerous for your baby. Keeping up her exercise routines for as long as she feels comfortable is as good for her mental health as it is for her physical.

Ensure that her instructor is aware she's pregnant. It's not always obvious; inform them of any physical limitations your partner may have. If Mum has been doing yoga before becoming pregnant, then keep it going. If she's new to yoga, then it's probably sensible to discuss this with your midwife or doctor first. If your partner is keen to start yoga, maybe suggest that she find a qualified local teacher with experience teaching pregnant women. The best endorsement would be from any of her friends with children who did yoga while they were pregnant.

This isn't a complete list, but here are some of the positions from my research that are best to be avoided during pregnancy:

- Lying on her back
- Crunches or sit-ups
- Forward fold with her feet together
- Twisting postures
- Deep back bends
- Inversions
- Hot yoga

**If unsure, make sure she asks her doctor for advice. It almost certainly won't be the first time her midwife has been asked this from an expectant mum keen to keep herself and her unborn baby happy and healthy.*

How Can You Support Your Partner, Baby & Yourself In Week 19?

Your partner may want to exercise alone to give herself some head space or prefer to exercise with other pregnant ladies.

That said, if she's keen to do some exercise together, going for a walk is an excellent thing for you both. Here are a few suggestions for ensuring it stays safe and effective for you, her and your baby.

This may be frustrating if she's previously used to intense exercise, but it's not a good idea for her to exhaust herself. A good guide is that she should be able to converse with you as you exercise together. If your pregnant partner wasn't partaking in strenuous exercise before pregnancy, she shouldn't suddenly take it up now. If I was asked to suggest one exercise, it would be walking together in the country-side. I say this largely because of what it will do to boost both your mental and physical health.

Chapter Takeaways

1. Exercise does not have to be strenuous to be beneficial.
2. Yoga is safe for pregnant women if the instructor is well-trained, qualified and experienced in training pregnant participants.
3. Going for a walk where she can maintain a

conversation with you will benefit your physical and mental well-beings as well as strengthening your relationship.

"When you teach your son, you teach your son's son."

- The Talmud (The Central Text of Rabbinic Judaism)

Chapter 20
Week 20

What Actually Happens At The 20-Week Scan?

Although both the 12 & 20-week scans are important in different ways, the 20-week scan was the big one for me. We got much more information about our baby, including its gender, at the 20-week scan. This may differ from country to country, but our NHS scan was carried out by a trained medical person called a sonographer. The scan takes place in a dimly lit room, I imagine making it easier to get a good look at your baby on the monitor.

Your partner will be asked to lie on the hospital couch and lower her clothing to hip level. She'll need to lift the top half of her clothing, so her tummy is uncovered. The sonographer or assistant will protect her clothing with tissue paper so as not to get any gel anywhere other than your partner's tummy. The sonographer then sweeps a handheld probe that looks like a cross between a TV remote and a torch over your partner's tummy to examine your baby's body. This then produces a black-and-white image of your baby on the ultrasound screen.

According to my wife, it didn't hurt, but the sonographer may have to apply a bit of pressure to get the best look at the baby, and this can feel uncomfortable but apparently not painful.

How Can You Support Your Partner, Baby & Yourself In Week 20?

Regarding what you need to do, just be as present as you can and take it all in. If like myself, you sometimes struggle to feel present or even really understand what it means, here are five suggestions.

- Take notice of your surroundings, in this case the room you're in. Try and focus on the details of objects around you, in this case maybe the monitor showing an image of your son or daughter. What exactly can you see, hear, smell, and feel?
- Try and focus on one thing at a time. For example, open and close your hand and notice the colour, the lines, or any distinguishing marks. How does it feel to stretch your hands or squeeze them when you make a fist?

- Take a moment to be consciously grateful for what you have today. Not what you hope for in the future but what you have and where you are now. In this case, a man sitting in a hospital room looking at an image of your son or daughter. As life defining moments go, this will be up there. There are millions of people who would give their right arm to be where you are. You can have all the money, power or social status in the world but getting the opportunity to be someone's mum or dad is a privilege that's not bestowed on everyone.
- Accept situations as they are as opposed to what you would prefer them to be. Try and remember that there may have been a previous version of you that dreamt to be living the life you are experiencing today.
- Do some daily deep breathing exercises. As previously mentioned, this is a great way to calm yourself down. It's also a great way to feel more present.

I held my wife's hand and just enjoyed the experience of seeing our daughter. You may have a million questions, but it might help the sonographer to keep quiet until she's finished with the probe and has completed all the checks.

How Long Does It Take?

The scan itself takes about 30 minutes, but this isn't something you should try and shoehorn into a lunch break.

My advice, if possible, is to take the day off. You don't want to be preoccupied with thoughts about parking tickets running out, or your boss ringing to ask where you are?

My wife had her heart set on finding out the sex, but typically our baby was lying in an awkward position with its legs crossed.

Regarding wanting to know the sex, which, if the baby doesn't want to turn around, isn't always possible, ask the sonographer at the beginning of the appointment that, if possible, you'd really like to know the sex. According to the NHS website, some hospitals can refuse to tell you the sex of the baby.

Survival Tip

There's no legal requirement to attend the 20-week scan, but it's not something that anyone should ideally have to do alone. The 20-week scan can sometimes show that the baby has a health condition, and unquestionably this type of news would be much harder to process on your own. I've attended three 20-week scans and am glad I did.

I found it to be a unique and exciting experience. It's an excellent opportunity to demonstrate to your partner how you're supporting her and going to smash it at being a dad.

The 20-week scan will gather information about the baby's heart, brain, bones, spinal cord, kidneys, and abdomen. It also allows the sonographer to look for the following (*rare*) conditions:

- Patau's syndrome
- Edwards' syndrome
- Lethal skeletal dysplasia
- Bilateral renal agenesis
- Serious cardiac abnormalities
- Exomphalos
- Gastroschisis
- Diaphragmatic hernia
- Cleft lip
- Open spina bifida
- Anencephaly

In most cases, you are told any relevant results there and then. If the scan indicates that something might need further investigation, you will be offered another test. You would then be given more information about the test so you can decide if you do or don't want it. This is something you could discuss with your midwife.

What's Happening Inside At The 20-Week Stage?

Your baby's skin is now covered in a slippery white substance called vernix. It's like an organic moisturiser for babies that protects the skin while in the amniotic fluid. Around the 20-week stage, your partner may develop a dark line down the middle of her tummy. This is a normal development of her skin pigmentation when her tummy expands to accommodate the growing baby bump. It's called the linea nigra.

Does The Linea Nigra Serve A Purpose?

Apparently not. If you ask an old wife who's fond of a tale, she may tell you it's because newborn babies can only tell light and dark. The darker skin of the "linea nigra" can help to guide them to the also darker skin of nipples to get their milk.

Chapter Takeaways

1. Make sure to attend the 20-week scan. It will show your partner you're the man for the job and reassure her that you're going to be a great dad.

2. I suggest waiting till the sonographer has completed the scan and taken the measurements before asking questions.
3. The 20-week scan felt like a big moment as it dawned on me that I would soon be someone's dad. This can feel daunting; if it does, confide in a friend or sibling instead of your partner. She may feel equally daunted and having to shoulder your fears may therefore be a bit of an ask.

"My father used to play with my brother and me in the yard. Mother would come out and say, 'You're tearing up the grass.' 'We're not raising grass,' Dad would reply. 'We're raising boys.'"

- American Baseball Legend Harmon Killebrew

Chapter 21
Week 21

How Do I Ease My Partner's Concerns About How Much Movement She Feels?

Baby movements start off as delicate little flutters. Eventually, they will become kicks that are so clear you can just about count the change in your child's back pocket! It's easier to feel your baby's movements if it's not your first baby; you're less likely to write it off as wind. If it's your first baby, you may feel movements from the 18 to the 20-week stage. If you're a seasoned pro on your second, third etc., you might feel movements a week or two earlier.

Regarding how often you should feel kicks, it depends entirely on your baby. Your partner will get used to the movement and will feel them up until they are born.

How Can You Support Your Partner, Baby & Yourself In Week 21 Onwards?

We were advised that if your partner thinks the baby is moving less than usual or there are other changes to what has become your baby's regular schedule, then call the midwife or maternity unit immediately.

I remember one occasion, getting up in the middle of the night because my wife was worried about the lack of baby movement she had felt that day. We called the maternity unit and were instructed to come straight in. As "*team support*," this is just another opportunity to step up. I assure you neither of you will be getting any sleep until she's satisfied that your baby is happy and healthy.

Your baby will need to be checked by professionals, do not use and trust a handheld scanning device, as these are unreliable. Having to work as a team to support your children even before they are born is excellent practice for the nocturnal life you're about to embark on. By 21 weeks, your baby weighs around 350g which is the same as a grown man's heart or a tin of Campbell's soup. It's also now heavier than the placenta.

This extra weight puts a lot of pressure on your partner's back. To support her, encourage her to keep doing exercise.

Survival Tip

Be part of the solution, not the problem. If your partner is understandably anxious that she hasn't felt her baby kick, keep a lid on your own emotions. Instead of sharing anxiety, be the daddy and take control. You were designed to rule in situations like this.

Don't ask questions she probably can't answer. Just remain calm, decide on a plan, and then act on the plan. Instead of self-diagnosing, call the maternity ward so they are expecting you, get in the car and get your partner the reassurance she needs. She can only get this reassurance from a trained medical professional, not you or the internet.

Chapter Takeaways

1. Your partner will get used to the frequency of your baby's movements. Call the maternity ward or your midwife to get professional medical advice if she is ever concerned that she hasn't felt much movement.
2. Take your partner's concerns very seriously, even if it's 2 a.m. and you're working in the morning. You would never forgive yourself if you poo-poohed her concerns and something went wrong.
3. Your baby is getting heavier than the placenta, heart, and soup tins. Ensure you encourage your

partner to keep up the exercise to maintain her fitness and strength.

"He didn't tell me how to live; he lived and let me watch him do it."

- American Writer Clarence Budington Kelland

Chapter 22
Week 22

Will My Child Be Born With Hair?

Many experts believe what determines whether a child is born with hair is influenced by its parent's genes and ethnicity.

That said, what does happen around this stage concerning body hair is quite interesting. The baby becomes covered in a layer of fine hair called *lanugo*. This hair disappears before it's born at around the 28-week stage. Its purpose isn't completely understood. Some experts believe it helps to regulate the baby's body temperature.

How Can You Support Your Partner, Baby & Yourself In Week 22?

At this stage, your baby will start to get into something resembling a sleep and awake pattern. This is almost certainly the exact opposite of your partner's or yours. One of the best things you can do to support your partner, who might be being kept awake by a restless baby, is:

1. Not make a fuss about her inability to sleep contributing to your inability to sleep.
2. Let her have the bed and decamp to either a spare room if you have one or the sofa. She will feel more relaxed alone, especially if she is aware her being awake is keeping you awake.

Something else that can happen around the 22-week stage is that your partner gets stretch marks on her stomach, breasts, and thighs. Depending on her skin colour, they can be pink, red, purple, or brown. They can fade and become less noticeable but may make your partner feel self-conscious. If your partner's self-esteem is taking a bit of a battering at this time, the addition of having stretch marks won't help.

Survival Tip

Don't be grumpy about sleeping on the sofa because your partner is being kept awake by baby gymnastics. Look for the positives, celebrate your situation and create yourself a cosy man den. A comfortable sofa where you can fidget & scroll through your phone without fear of being told off by your other half.

Chapter Takeaways

1. If your partner is being kept awake by a wriggly unborn baby, I would advise you to offer to move to the sofa. To avoid her worrying, make it clear your sole reason for doing this is to give her more space.
2. Your partner may start getting stretch marks on her breasts, baby bump or thighs. This can potentially make her feel self-conscious. This may be a good week to action a full charm offensive to remind her just how awesome she is. Not only for growing and looking after your baby but how much you love her for doing so.

"A truly rich man is one whose children run into his arms when his hands are empty."

- Anonymous

Chapter 23
Week 23

What Are Haemorrhoids?

Developing piles (*haemorrhoids*) is a common thing for women to have to deal with during pregnancy. Haemorrhoids are swellings containing enlarged blood vessels in or around the bottom (*rectum anus area*). They're not exclusive to pregnant women and can affect anyone. They can be extremely uncomfortable, and people are often embarrassed about having them because of where they are.

Why Do Women Get Piles During Pregnancy?

There are certain hormones produced in your partner's body that make piles more likely. The hormone progesterone relaxes the walls of your partner's blood vessels, increasing the chances of someone developing haemorrhoids.

As the baby grows and gets heavier, it puts more pressure on your partner's veins. This not only encourages the development of piles but also constipation—double nightmare!

How Can You Support Your Partner, Baby & Yourself In Week 23?

As previously mentioned, not only can having piles be very uncomfortable, especially when your partner is trying to do a poo, they're something she may be self-conscious about. As well as being painful, other symptoms of piles can be bleeding or traces of blood after doing a poo. Your bottom can also become very itchy. There may also be a discharge of mucus after visiting the loo. As I'm sure you can imagine, having piles is miserable, but there are things you can do to help. Make sure she drinks enough fluids and stays well-hydrated. By fluids, I mean water as opposed to tea or coffee. Tea and coffee are diuretics which will make her more dehydrated. Being dehydrated will make doing a poo much more painful.

Regular exercise like a brisk daily walk will improve her circulation and raise her mood. Encouraging her to eat a diet that's both high in fibre and contains plenty of fruit and veg will help too.

Survival Tip

Buying the cheap and cheerful (*sand papery*) loo roll may save you a couple of quid but may antagonise your partner's sore bum. Take the hit and treat her to some quilted 3-ply shea butter and summer fruits fragranced bog roll.

Good luck suggesting this to your partner. If you do, perhaps do it via email to avoid getting a summer fruit-smelling loo roll to the side of the head. A damp tea towel that's been in the freezer for 30 mins can help to relieve soreness and itchiness around her bum hole.

It might also help her to wipe her bum with fragrance-free wet wipes as opposed to toilet tissue. Keeping these wet wipes in the fridge can help to further reduce any pain. Her doctor or midwife may suggest or prescribe medication or ointment to help soothe any soreness.

Having piles is a very common condition during pregnancy but having them doesn't pose any sort of danger to your baby. It's a condition that usually clears up in the days or weeks following birth. However, if for whatever reason it doesn't, then your partner should mention it to her doctor or midwife.

Chapter Takeaways

1. Your partner may struggle with piles during her pregnancy. There's not a massive amount you can do apart from buying the softest loo roll you can find.
2. Encouraging her to get regular exercise can help boost her circulation, which can help with constipation and, in turn, piles.
3. Your partner staying hydrated will help to reduce the pain when she needs to do a poo.

"I have found the best way to give advice to your children is to find out what they want and then advise them to do it."

- Ex US President Harry S Truman

Chapter 24
Week 24

At What Week Could The Baby Be Born?

This stage of pregnancy signifies the time if a child was to be born now, at 24 weeks, it would have a chance of survival, even though it's still about 16 to 18 weeks until the due date. Sadly, children born before this are unlikely to survive because their lungs and several other vital organs will not have developed enough. At 24 weeks, your child is now 11 and a half inches long and weighs about 1 pound. That's about the same size as an ear of corn.

How Can You Support Your Partner, Baby & Yourself In Week 24?

There will continue to be changes to your partner's body that might make her feel self-conscious or unsettled. Instead of commenting on how she looks huge, massive, or enormous, tell her how beautiful she is and how she really suits being pregnant. She almost certainly won't believe you but may appreciate the effort.

Around this week, her belly button, if it was an innie, will now become an outie. Her navel should return to its previous shape after she's given birth. Your partner may experience swelling in her joints during pregnancy. This swelling can cause fluids to gather in her lower half. When she's lying down, these fluids can be moved to the rest of her body. This can result in a dull ache in her fingers, hands or wrists. As well as encouraging her to rest, you could get her an ice pack which may reduce the swelling and pain in her wrists or hands.

Regarding her hands, your partner may get red, itchy palms during her pregnancy. She may also experience a metallic taste in her mouth, larger feet and skin tags appearing during this 24-week stage. If she does suffer from red itchy palms, it's worth her mentioning it to the doctor, as there is always a chance that it could indicate a rare pregnancy complication called cholestasis of pregnancy. This complication would more likely appear in the 3rd trimester (26 weeks to 40 weeks), but it's wise to mention it to her doctor or midwife.

What Is Cholestasis Of Pregnancy?

This is a liver disease due to the flow of bile being affected because her pregnancy hormones are produced. Women with this condition can experience severe itching on their hands, feet, and other areas of the body. Other symptoms can include a dark colour to urine, a yellowing of her skin and the whites of her eyes. If your partner is experiencing new, severe, or persistent symptoms, she should contact her healthcare provider (GP or midwife) asap.

Survival Tip

If you are still sharing a bed, don't get cross about what might seem like an excessive number of cushions or pillows. For the reasons explained in this chapter, your partner may have sore joints and need a complex arrangement of pillows and cushions to feel comfortable. If it's annoying you, sleep on the sofa, thankful for the knowledge that none of your joints hurt.

Chapter Takeaways

1. Your baby is now getting heavier, which puts increased pressure on your partner's body. Try to get her to rest whenever she can.
2. If she has concerns about aches and pains in her wrists and hands, she should discuss this with her midwife.
3. If your partner shows any of the symptoms associated with cholestasis of pregnancy (ICP): severe itching on her hands, feet, and other areas of her body, dark colour to their urine or yellowing of the skin and whites of her eyes, then you need to contact her midwife or GP ASAP.

"I believe that what we become depends on what our fathers teach us at odd moments when they aren't trying to teach us."

- Italian Historian Umberto Eco

Chapter 25
Week 25

Why Are My Partner's Feet Getting Bigger During Pregnancy?

Women's feet and hands can swell during pregnancy because of water retention. It's another reason you should encourage your partner to try and put her feet up whenever she can.

Your partner should mention any swelling she has to her midwife to be on the safe side. This will allow the midwife to check her blood pressure and rule out a serious condition called pre-eclampsia.

What's Pre-Eclampsia?

It's a dangerous condition that raises blood pressure and will show traces of protein in her urine. The exact cause is unknown, but medical professionals suspect it's linked to improper functioning of the placenta. They also believe it can be caused by a high fat or a nutritionally poor diet, insufficient blood flow to the placenta or genetic factors. The best ways are to help your partner to get lots of rest. Add little to no salt to her meals and drink 6 to 8 glasses of water a day. If she also regularly exercises and avoids fatty, fried foods and drinks with high levels of caffeine, that will help.

How Can You Support Your Partner, Baby & Yourself In Week 25?

Make sure she gets lots of rest, eats well and avoids caffeine. If her resting more means you're stuck on washing up detail for the next 15 weeks or so, buy some nice marigolds and embrace it.

You could start buying and joining her in drinking decaf coffee or tea to show more support. Try to keep her hydrated by investing in one of those water bottles that show how much water you have consumed. It can help to have a target.

Survival Tip

As tempting as it is to make jokes about your partner's giant feet, I'd advise against it. Any references to your wife turning into "Big Foot" or suggesting she asks to borrow Andre the Giant's or a retired clown's flip-flops will probably go down like a cup of cold sick.

Chapter Takeaways

1. Your partner's feet and hands may swell due to water retention; encouraging her to take lots of rest will help.
2. Support her in keeping hydrated by doing so yourself. Invest in a water bottle that shows you how much water you have drunk in litres etc.
3. Cut down on drinks high in caffeine, like coffee and tea, or by buying decaffeinated versions.

"Dad is and always will be my living, breathing superhero."

- Bindi Irwin (Daughter Of The Late Australian Zookeeper Steve Irwin)

Chapter 26
Week 26

When Can Our Baby Open Their Eyes And What Colour Will They Be?

Your baby's eyelids will start to open for the first time around the 26-week stage. You may have heard that all babies are born with blue eyes, but this isn't the case. Eye colour is determined by the eye colour genes found in chromosome 15. It can also be affected by other genes.

Many of the genes linked with eye colour are involved in the movement, production and storage of a pigment called melanin. A baby's eye colour is directly related to the amount of melanin present in the front layers of the area of the eye called the iris. The iris is the coloured area of your eye.

Children born with brown eyes will have a large amount of melanin in their iris compared to children with blue eyes, who will have much less.

Two brown-eyed parents don't mean you will automatically have a brown-eyed child. Two of our three children have similar "brown" eye colours to us, but our youngest has blue eyes. Our postman also has blue eyes, but my wife said that's just a coincidence.

How Can You Support Your Partner, Baby & Yourself In Week 26?

It will be suggested to your partner that she should have a whooping cough vaccination anytime between the 16 and 32-week stage of her pregnancy. She must ask her midwife or GP if she still needs to do this. Since you are now in the third and final trimester, it might be worth thinking about creating a birth plan.

A birth plan is a precise, often bullet-pointed, often one-page document of your partner's preferences for the birth of her baby.

It's a useful thing to have created as it will give any medical staff involved an idea of what support you want. It will also give your partner a chance to start mentally preparing for what will be one, if not the most significant physical and mental challenge of her life. If she needs help with creating her birth plan, her midwife can provide some support.

Having researched it, the NHS offers a comprehensive birth plan that you can download from their website. The birth plan will include general information like your partner's name, due date, where she would like to give birth, etc.

It will also let you provide information about what sort of pain relief she might prefer. If she wants to move around doing labour.

If she wants to be calmed with whale music or inspired by drum and base. It's worth checking out the downloadable document on the NHS website. Their birth plan template may enlighten you, as it did for me, on some elements of the birthing process you never realised were an option.

For example:

- Would you like certain religious customs to be observed?
- Would you like to try breastfeeding straight away or pass him or her to Dad for some bottle feeding?
- What are your plans for the placenta?
- How does your partner feel about the possible need to have an episiotomy?

I can only imagine like running a flipping mile!

What's An Episiotomy?

An episiotomy when the midwife or doctor needs to make a cut in your partner's perineum (the area between the vagina and the anus). This is done to make the opening of her vagina a bit wider and easier for the baby to pass through.

If you end up watching this happen and you're anything like me, this might be one of, if not the primary, reasons you're in total awe of how courageous and brave she is.

Don't be surprised if you are suddenly overcome with a wave of pure love and admiration for her at this moment. Having to deal with this basically makes her a total rockstar for life!

Survival Tip

If I ever feel hard done by in regard to something my wife has or hasn't done, I just need to say the word "episiotomy" and that's the trigger I need to wind my own neck in. The recall of that memory and the way my wife apologised for apologising to the midwife when she flinched in what can only have been toe-curling pain is a constant reason why I'm never really in a good position to complain about having a bit of a cold or having to take some recycling out.

Chapter Takeaways

1. If your partner still needs to get a whooping cough vaccination, it needs to be done, ideally between the 16 and 32-week stages.
2. Even though your partner's due date is probably 14 weeks away, the baby could arrive early. With that in mind, it might be a good time to create a birth plan. Your midwife can advise you on this, and you can download an excellent birth plan template from the NHS website.

"A father carries pictures where his money used to be."

- American Actor & Comedian Steve Martin

Chapter 27
Week 27

Why Does My Partner Sometimes Wee Herself?

Being pregnant and giving birth can significantly weaken the muscles of your partner's pelvic floor. She may notice this by leaking a bit of wee when she coughs, sneezes, or laughs at her partner stepping on a Lego brick in the middle of the night.

What Is The Pelvic Floor?

Your pelvic floor is the figure of eight shaped muscle that can stretch like a hammock from the end of the spine to your pubic bone. It's the muscle responsible for stopping your wee mid-flow, which is not an easy skill.

Like all muscles, it can be developed and strengthened. Your partner having a strong pelvic floor will stop her from weeing herself if she's doing star jumps or crying with laughter because her husband mistook a no-entry sign for an end-of-national-speed-limit sign! I know, hysterical! She doesn't get out much these days.

How Can You Support Your Partner, Baby & Yourself In Week 27?

Doing pelvic floor exercises will strengthen the muscles around the bladder, bottom, vagina, and penis. At this stage, sex may be wishful thinking, but a strong pelvic floor can create stiffer erections, stronger orgasms, and increased levels of sensitivity. With that in mind, it's worth adding it to your weekly workout schedule.

Survival Tip

Warning: this is so much easier said than done. If, for whatever reason—like piles, constipation, tiredness or nausea—your partner isn't in the mood for sex, try not to offload that sexual frustration onto her.

This is painfully hard—excuse the pun—and I'm not sure there is much of a way around it. Try cold showers or taking matters into your own hands, if you catch my drift.

To activate your pelvic floor muscles, imagine yourself stopping yourself from having a wee. According to my oracle for this book, the NHS website, it's not advised to frequently try and stop your wee flow midstream as it can harm your bladder.

Suggested Pelvic Floor Exercise

Sit in a comfortable position and squeeze the muscle 10 to 15 times. Make sure not to hold your breath or tighten your stomach, bum, or thigh muscles simultaneously. After you have mastered it, try holding each pelvic floor squeeze for a couple of seconds.

Like any exercise, be careful not to overdue and have a rest in between sets. Why not try some while you're waiting for the kettle to boil or in any queue?

What's Happening Inside At The 27-Week Stage?

At this stage, your baby's heart rate, which is still much faster than yours, will have slowed to about 140 beats per minute. His or her digestive system, lungs and brain are formed but have not finished developing.

Chapter Takeaways

1. If your partner still needs to book a whooping cough vaccination, remind her to do so ASAP.

2. This is her call, so don't be pushy, but if she hasn't downloaded and started thinking about creating a birth plan, now would be a good time to suggest it.
3. Do pelvic floor exercises to help your partner with her piddling problems.

"The loss of my father will always sting. But now everything I do is in honour of him and celebrates his life."

- Adrienne C Moore, *Orange Is the New Black* Star

Chapter 28
Week 28

How's The Baby Doing?

At this stage in your partner's pregnancy, your baby weighs about 1kg. That's the equivalent of a litre of water, a pineapple, or eight apples.

More importantly, they are formed at this stage but will continue to put on more weight until they are born. Our children (1 and 3) went full term by arriving around 42 weeks and weighed between 3 and 3.5kg at birth. Our middle son, born early at 38 weeks, weighed closer to 2.5kg.

Your midwife or GP will be able to hear your baby's heartbeat with the help of a stethoscope. You can listen to it if you place your ear on your partner's bump.

How Can You Support Your Partner, Baby & Yourself In Week 28?

You can help by staying helpful, proactive, loving, and cheerful. Keep up the exercise, do all the housework, encourage her to rest, keep her well-hydrated and provide her with lots of good nutrition.

Why Does My Partner Keep Getting Nosebleeds?

Your partner's—and everyone's—nose is full of tiny blood vessels. These blood vessels can get dried out from normal breathing, resulting in them breaking and bleeding. Your partner getting nosebleeds during pregnancy is standard; nine times out of ten, there's no reason to worry. Most nosebleeds are due to increased blood volume and, in your partner's case, hormonal changes in her body.

How Can You Stop A Nosebleed?

The first and most important thing is to remain calm. You can do this by concentrating on or even counting your inhale and exhale breaths.

The sight of your own blood or, for some people, any blood can be enough to make them feel panicky. To effectively manage a nosebleed, sit up straight, maintain an upright posture, and pinch your nostrils together. You don't need to put your head between your legs; a slight incline is enough to stop a nosebleed.

If your partner finds that she is having frequent or severe nosebleeds, she needs to talk to her GP or midwife so they can rule out any other potential complications.

How Can We Calm Down When Panicking?

Regarding what is generally considered good advice, taking one or several deep breaths may not actually help to calm you or your partner down.

Taking deep breaths or gulps of oxygen is linked to the sympathetic nervous system. That's the clever system in the body that controls your "fight or flight" response. This is the part of your brain that summons the strength required to lift a car if a child is trapped. For pre-historic man, outrun a sabre tooth tiger or, in the case of modern man, run for the number 27.

Taking lots of deep breaths and, therefore, lots of oxygen, can cause you to hyperventilate, which can worsen the situation.

Instead, trying to lengthen your exhale can be much more effective. For example, breathe in for a count of 2 or 3 and breathe out for a count of 4 or 5. Your body's ability to exhale is linked to the parasympathetic nervous system. This system's job is to help you relax and calm down.

Survival Tip

If you struggle with the sight of blood, practice the breathing technique above. There is absolutely no shame (as I keep telling myself) in fainting at the sight of blood. Even if that results in a trainee midwife having to hold a fan above your head as your second child is in an actual state of arrival.

It won't help her if you spin out when things start getting messy. If you can spend some time preparing yourself through calm breathing practice, it may help you both.

Chapter Takeaways

1. Nose bleeds during pregnancy are normal. If they become severe or frequent, your partner should contact her midwife.
2. If you get panicky at the sight of blood, practice remaining calm with the suggested breathing techniques. You have absolutely got this!
3. Your partner will probably have a 28-week appointment with her midwife or doctor. This is a

good opportunity for her to ask questions. At this appointment, they will most likely measure her blood pressure, take a sample of her wee to test it for protein and discuss the results of any previous screening tests.

"She did not stand alone, but what stood behind her, the most potent moral force in her life, was the love of her father." (Extract from *Go Set a Watchman*)

- American Novelist Harper Lee

Chapter 29
Week 29

How Many Baby Movements A Day Is The Standard Number Of Baby Movements?

Every pregnancy is entirely unique to the women experiencing it. There is no "normal" number. There is only whatever normal has become for your partner and her baby.

Suppose your baby's movement pattern changes to the extent that your partner is aware or concerned about it. In that case, she should contact her midwife or the maternity ward straight away to get some professional advice.

How Can You Support Your Partner, Baby & Yourself In Week 29?

As your baby develops, he or she may start to push up against Mum's lungs. This, plus the extra weight of your baby (8 apples or 1 pineapple), can make your partner feel breathless.

This feeling of breathlessness might make your partner feel anxious. This ironically might then make her more anxious and breathless about being anxious and breathless. If this is the case, I suggest trying the breathing techniques suggested in the last chapter. If she is being stubborn or in a state or heightened anxiety where she can't engage, you might need to lead her into breathing techniques. Your baby's weight gain can tire your partner out, and she needs to listen to her body and get as much rest as her body tells her it needs. This might be difficult to encourage someone to do, especially as she may be nesting at this point in her pregnancy.

What Is Nesting?

It's basically as it sounds. Birds, other animals, and pregnant women are driven by an urge to create a safe and clean environment for their offspring. The desire to sort the habitat kicks in around the 28 weeks. In this, the third and final trimester, her body is starting to prepare for birth.

Her brain is getting ready by wanting to prepare the home or nest for the new family member's arrival.

This may sound like an old wife's tale. As someone who was obsessed with painting skirting boards in the summer of 2012, I can assure you "nesting" is a thing. It's also a thing that may affect you just as much as your partner. It seems like a bit of a cruel move from Mother Nature to suddenly provide a pregnant lady with a sudden burst of energy and desire to clean, tidy, and paint everything in her home. If this describes your partner's behaviour, don't worry; she is nesting, which is a natural state for either of you to be in at this stage.

Survival Tip

If you suspect your partner is nesting, I advise against criticising her for rushing around and not doing what you think she should, which is resting. Very little is stronger than her maternal instinct to prepare a home for her baby. Getting in the way may result in being cleaned, painted, varnished, or laminated.

I would try to embrace it and get yourself involved. If you help and do half of the work, you will not only be helping her but strengthening your bond.

What Signs Will Indicate My Partner Is Nesting?

It's not an exact science and will differ slightly from person to person. Your partner may decide one day that she wants to clean, tidy and re-organise your home. She may also become more selective about the company she keeps. She may prefer to spend more time at home and only with people she knows or trusts. You may also become more selective about who you see and socialise with, preferring to spend time with people you trust and stay at home more.

If your partner doesn't overdo it, there is no risk with nesting. I advise you both to take full advantage of this newfound energy and get your house in order. Don't question it, don't worry about it, just use it.

Chapter Takeaways

1. Your partner may feel breathless because of the size of her baby pushing against her lungs. To avoid getting stressed or anxious, practice the breathing techniques suggested in chapter 28.
2. If your partner is nesting, don't get frustrated that she won't chill out and rest. Instead, roll your sleeves up and help her.

First Time Dad

"My dad's my best mate, and he always will be."

- British Pop Star Cher Lloyd

Chapter 30
Week 30

Is Our Baby Still Covered in All That Fine Furry Hair?

No, the soft fine hair called lanugo that will have covered your baby up to this point, and the white greasy (vernix) substance is starting to disappear.

How Can I Support My Partner, Our Baby and Myself at This Stage?

You can get down to what might be week 1 of a 6 or 8-week antenatal course.

These courses are often free for new parents (the NHS provides free classes). The course in Brighton UK that we did was interesting, good fun, full of great advice and provided biscuits. I also found it helpful to meet other men who were about to become dads like me.

Survival Tip

Life is a lot like laundry; the more you put in, the more you get out. If you sit at antenatal classes with your arms crossed, with a face like a slapped arse because you're missing your five-a-side football, don't be surprised if you get a very cold shoulder from your partner. We have three children but only went to antenatal classes for our first. As you may have picked up from the general tone, I'm a cynical person most of the time.

That said, the classes did make it feel more exciting and, like the 20-week scan, helped me prepare mentally. You may not make lifelong friends; I've only got 2 friends and struggle to see them on an annual basis. For my wife, meeting other mums who were due on the same day or very close seemed to be a genuine support for her.

My Partner Is Struggling To Get To Sleep!

The size of your partner's bump may now make it very hard for her to get comfortable when she's lying down. Leg cramps are a common problem from the 29 to the 32-week stage.

If you are still sharing a bed, you might find her bump is getting too big for either of you to get a good night's sleep.

Mum may find the only way she's comfy is by being supported by a carefully balanced Jenga-like system of pillows and scatter cushions. You may demolish her finely constructed cushion tower if you roll over and accidentally move one. Moving to the sofa might ensure any middle-of-the-night cushion accidents don't end up demolishing your relationship. From memory, if your partner lays curled up on her side in a foetal position with one or several pillows between her legs and a cushion or an L-shaped pillow surrounding and supporting her bump, she may be able to get comfy.

Chapter Takeaways

1. Make an effort and attend an antenatal class. You might not be that into it, but the woman growing your child probably is. She may also be getting a lot of comfort from being a part of this unique community, not to mention all the relevant information that's being provided.
2. Through these antenatal classes, your partner can join a very close-knit group of women. Women who are all going through the same experience within days of each other, who may live less than a bus ride apart.

3. If your partner struggles to get comfy at night, move onto the sofa. There is no guarantee that her 30 cleverly positioned pillows will help her to sleep, but at least she won't blame you, maybe!

"A father holds his daughter's hand for a short while, but he holds her heart forever."

- Anonymous

Chapter 31
Week 31

How Big Is Our Baby At This Stage?

Your baby continues to put on size and weight. He or she will be about 15 inches long from head to heel; that's the specification for a bowling pin. They will weigh about 1 and a half kg, equivalent to a coconut. Your baby will be increasingly active, doing somersaults and probably giving you some great "Was that a heel?" moments. They will also be learning to suck their thumb, no doubt in preparation for breastfeeding.

How Can You Support Your Partner, Baby & Yourself In Week 31?

It's not uncommon for your partner to get an itchy stomach around this time. She may also feel itchy in other areas, like her bum or boobs. The best way to deal with it, apart from treating her to a good scratch, is to encourage her to drink lots of water and apply moisturiser to the itchy areas.

Your partner's baby bump may be making it increasingly tiring for her to move around. If you have the time and resources to drive and collect her to and from midwife appointments as opposed to her walking or having to take public transport, that would be a good idea. One consistency of appointments from now on will be checking her blood pressure. This is because high blood pressure can be an early sign of pre-eclampsia.

What Is Braxton Hicks?

Mum may feel her bump tighten for 20 to 30 seconds, then relax; this tightening shouldn't hurt. For want of a better word, these are "practice" contractions. Braxton Hicks contractions are entirely normal. If they start to become painful or your partner gets them regularly, it could be a sign of early labour. If that happens, advise her to contact her midwife.

Survival Tip

I would never refer to these contractions as "practice" as I imagine they feel real to her.

If your partner is having what you think could be Braxton Hicks as opposed to full contractions, but she wants to check she's not in labour, you need to allow her the time to make the call on that. Don't diagnose something that is happening in her body, not yours.

With that in mind, make sure you both have the names and numbers of her midwife, GP, and maternity ward on both of your phones. That way, if she's searching for that one thing she forgot to put in her hospital bag, you can be self-appointed mission control and do the comms for her.

Chapter Takeaways

1. If your partner has some itchiness on her stomach, breasts, or bum, encourage her to drink lots of water. You could also offer an agenda-free massage to get some moisturiser on those affected areas. You could offer to moisturise her back and neck and leave her responsible for moisturising her front to avoid any miscommunications.
2. If your partner has the sensation of her stomach tightening for 20-30 seconds, then relaxing, and it doesn't hurt, then it's likely to be the "practice contractions" Braxton Hicks. If they continue or are painful, *you* should ring her midwife ASAP.

3. Never refer to these contractions as "practice". It may become the punch line for future stories at dinner partners for the rest of your lives.

"My father has always provided me with a safe place to land and a hard place from which to launch."

- Chelsea Clinton (Bill & Hilary's Daughter)

Chapter 32
Week 32

Do I Have To Buy A Brand-New Pushchair?

Your partner's bump size and the weight of your baby continue to make it harder to walk, and her walking may now resemble more of a waddle.

From this week until week 36, your baby gains approximately 400 to 500 grams per week. They will put on about 1kg of extra fat reserves within that time frame. This fat is what helps them to stay warm after birth.

What's Happening Inside At The 32-Week Stage?

Your baby should be facing with its head down as it prepares for birth. Don't be alarmed when your midwife examines your partner that they find this isn't the case yet. If your baby isn't head down at 36 weeks, your midwife can suggest some techniques to move itself into the correct position for birth.

Your partner should be feeling the same frequencies of daily movements all the way to when she gives birth. If that activity reduces, she is best advised to contact her midwife ASAP.

Survival Tip

Your baby could be born any day now. If he or she arrived today and you had to collect your partner and baby from the hospital, could you? By that, I mean, do you have a pushchair yet?

Before you go out and buy the Rolls Royce of the pushchair world, take this in. A brand-new pushchair could set you back between £1200 and £1700!

After some research and trawling of several social media sites, we found a second-hand "Oyster" that had been kept in mint condition for £150. One of the hidden bonuses of becoming a parent is how much better the world seems to treat you. When I say the world, I specifically mean other parents. We ended up giving away lots of our kids' toys, clothes, and baby stuff once they were no longer needed.

Parents with even a few months more experience may seem happy to help anyone up to the next rung on the parenting ladder. If anyone offers you free clothes, toys, or pushchairs, and you need them, don't be proud; just accept it graciously. I found a bottle of wine or a box of chocolates to be a well-accepted exchange for their kindness.

Chapter Takeaways

1. Your partner's baby bump and size will make her walking more of a waddling.
2. She needs loads of rest and help from you.
3. If you still haven't bought a pushchair, you need one *now*, but don't buy a new one. You will be able to buy a second-hand one that's in good condition for about 10% of its original cost. Facebook Marketplace and Gumtree are full of parents with pushchairs they're trying to get rid of.

"When people look inside my life, I want to hear them say, 'She's got her father's eyes.' Her father's eyes that find the good in things when good is not around."

- Amy Grant, American Singer & Songwriter

Chapter 33
Week 33

How Much Caffeine Is Too Much During Pregnancy?

Too much caffeine isn't good for pregnant ladies or for your baby. It can increase the chance of a miscarriage or your baby being born at a low weight. If you're pregnant, the NHS website suggests not to have more than 200 milligrams of caffeine daily.

To put that into context. If you were to buy an 8-oz brewed coffee from Starbucks, there would be 180 milligrams of caffeine in it. If you were to have a single espresso, it would contain 75 milligrams of caffeine. The caffeine in a cup of black tea with milk is 47 milligrams.

How Can You Support Your Partner, Baby & Yourself In Week 33?

You will learn quickly that all your well-thought-out plans mean very little to your baby, who will arrive whenever they want. The statistic from *www.parents.com* that only 4 in every 100 babies arrives on their due date means that your partner must have her bag packed in case she goes into labour. In no order, I suggest making sure these items make it into her hospital bag.

- Wash bag and towel
- Your birth plan and any relevant hospital notes
- Something comfy and baggy to wear during labour. It might be worth wearing something she's not that precious about wearing again. That said, my wife still has all three of the maternity nighties. The 2012 vintage really doesn't owe her anything these days!
- Spare comfy clothes and underwear
- Baby grows for 3 to 4 days
- Dressing gown
- Newborn nappies (*they may look tiny but will probably swamp your newborn*)
- Baby bottles
- 2 to 3 formula milk cartons
- Nursing bras and breast pads
- Super absorbent sanitary pads

- Healthy snacks
- Unhealthy snacks
- A good book, although your baby might have other ideas
- Pain relief medication (*check with the midwives or nurses on duty*)
- Phone and charger

Survival Tip

The more of the "essential items" you can get into her hospital bag now, the fewer shuttle runs you may have to do to the nearest supermarket.

During the 48 hours post labour, your partner will have an absolute carte blanche to request you source any seemingly random items. Objects that somehow manage to drift into her fatigued subconscious will be on your next list.

Chocolate, grapes, flowers, a magazine, a two-speed breast pump, a dustpan and brush, a printer ink cartridge, a Daim bar or the lost treasure of the San Madre, etc.

What Is Group B Strep?

She will almost certainly be several steps ahead of you but asking her if she has asked her midwife about Group B strep shows you are taking your role seriously. Group B strep is a bacterium that up to 2 in every 5 people have in their body.

If you're carrying Group B strep while pregnant, there's a slight risk that it could make your baby very ill.

Chapter Takeaways

1. Your baby could arrive any day. If your partner hasn't sorted her bag, then now would be the time to do so. The list above suggests some, but not all, items you may need. The request for the lost treasure of the San Madre was a joke; the 2-speed breast pump wasn't!
2. If she hasn't asked her midwife about Group B strep, she should do so now.
3. Aiming to have no more than 200 milligrams of caffeine daily (ideally less) is a good idea during pregnancy.

"A girl's father is the first man in her life and probably the most influential."

- American Author David Jeremiah

Chapter 34
Week 34

What's The Soft Spot On The Baby's Head Called?

The soft spot on the baby's head is called the fontanelle, and it's the area of our baby's head that always made my legs feel funny when I accidentally touched it.

If you're like me, you may handle your baby as if he or she is made of porcelain. It's typical to be worried if you touch or brush over the fontanelle. This soft spot, on top of your newborn's head is covered by a thick membrane.

If you handle your child gently, your baby is in no danger. All your baby's bones will be hardening apart from the bones in the skull. These bones stay soft and separated until your partner has given birth. This is to make the baby's journey through the birth canal easier. Bones in the skull will gently slide over each other while still protecting your baby's brain.

The four and five-year-olds I help to coach Brazilian jiu-jitsu to are not babies. Of course, you should be careful when handling or picking up a child, but human beings are formidable. Being born is considered one of the most arduous physical experiences you go through in your lifetime. "Babies are tougher than they appear and won't 'break' with normal handling. While it's important to support their head until they have the neck strength to hold it up on their own, their head won't fall off if you forget. I promise! The biggest risks to your newborn are suffocation and infection," says Wendy Hasson, MD.

How Can You Support Your Partner, Baby & Yourself In Week 34?

Describing childbirth as "magical" is likely to make even the most dewy-eyed romantic roll their eyes, but from my experience, it kind of is.

Your partner may not share this sentiment, but I felt there was a sense that her body knew exactly what to do. Once the baby's head moves down into your partner's pelvis, which can happen at this stage, some of the pregnancy symptoms she's lived with for the past few months will disappear.

Your baby dropping down will naturally free up space in your partner's abdomen. This will relieve the constant pressure she has lived with on her lungs, making breathing feel easier. I imagine this, in turn, might make her feel calmer because she can breathe. This may also help with heartburn. If your partner is still at work, it might be time to clock out. The physical effort it may take to get to and from work might be exhausting for her.

This will depend on what she has discussed and agreed with her employer. If the baby arrives earlier than planned, her leave will start the day after she gives birth.

If she decides to take time off work due to pregnancy-related issues in the 4 weeks before her due date, her paid maternity leave will start then.

My partner worked right up to her due date with each of our 3 children. As a primary (elementary) school teacher, I imagine her birth plan was written, colour-coded, and laminated within hours of the 12-week scan!

There is no right or wrong time to stop working; it will differ from person to person. The easiest way to decide is to ask yourself what is best for the baby. Mum and baby are still the same physical entity, so is this also what's best for her?

If being at work is making her mentally or physically tired, she should stop. If it's helping to take her mind off birth-related anxiety, then maybe keep at it for a bit longer. I remember being in awe of my wife when I came home one day to find her in our kids' bedroom with a child under each arm reading *The Bear Snores On*.

Without context, this may not sound that impressive, but she was in the early stages of labour and pausing every couple of pages to breathe through another contraction. With your partner's work, if she wants to change the date when she starts her maternity leave, she will need to give her employer at least 28 days' notice in the UK.

Survival Tip

If your partner is like my wife, she may feel unnecessarily guilty about stopping work before the very moment she's pleading for gas and air. If this resonates, this might be your cue to step up, take control and give her permission to put herself first.

I wouldn't advise telling a pregnant woman or any woman that you're giving her permission to do...anything. You need to try and do this (verbally or non-verbally) because, from my experience, mums don't put themselves first. My wife often frustrates me by spending any Christmas or birthday money on our children or items for the house. She says it makes her happy, and my being frustrated is just something she views as a bonus.

I'm confident your partner will never look back and regret having stayed at work when she was tired and could've been resting at home on her maternity leave. I'm also confident that you will both do things as parents you never thought you'd ever be brave, capable, and strong enough to do.

Your partner should be sleeping on her side. If you're still trying to share a bed, I'd suggest decamping to the sofa and leaving her to swear at her cushion mountain in peace. Your partner sleeping on her side is best for her baby as it helps the blood flow to the placenta. Everything will feel bigger and heavier for your partner, including her breasts, which might also be leaking a yellowish liquid called colostrum. This liquid is the first round of milk. Colostrum is important as it's packed full of the antibodies your baby needs to protect it from diseases.

Chapter Takeaways

1. It might be worth practising the route from your house to the hospital. Tensions may be running high, and you don't want you getting lost like a big wally and compound the drama.
2. If your partner is still battling at work, remind her that her health is more critical than any

administrative task that could be handed over to a colleague.

3. When you see that soft spot, on top of your baby's head, don't panic. It's okay to touch and brush over it if you are gentle. The biggest thing to remember is to support your baby's head until its neck muscles are strong enough to support itself.
4. Encourage your wife to worry less about her house of cards cushion castle and more about sleeping on her side.

"No man I ever met was my father's equal, and I never loved any other man as much."

- American Actress Hedy Lamarr

Chapter 35
Week 35

How Big Is The Baby Now?

At this stage, your baby has done the lion's share of his or her development. They will be about 12.5 inches in length from the top of their head to the bottom of their bum. This is equivalent to the size of the sort of ruler you may have used at school. If you can't remember owning a ruler, it's also about the same length as a toaster.

The heel-to-head length is closer to 18 inches. This is about the same length as a rolling pin, a windshield wiper blade and a giraffe's tongue.

What Happens If My Baby Is Born This Week?

If your partner was to go into labour and give birth this week or next (before week 37), it would be considered a premature birth.

If a baby is born early, it may need to spend time in the hospital's special care unit. Our middle one was born at 36 weeks and had to spend a few days in the Trevor Mann unit at Brighton General. He's a very healthy eight-year-old who's obsessed with Brighton & Hove Football club, and jiu-jitsu. He also has the appetite of a small horse.

How Can You Support Your Partner, Baby & Yourself In Week 35?

Your partner may get headaches in the first and third trimesters. In the 3rd trimester, she may also struggle to sleep. Anything you can do to help her with these 2 specific issues will help.

Is She Allowed To Take Paracetamol During Pregnancy?

According to my oracle for this book, the NHS website, paracetamol is safe for pregnant women in most cases. They state, "It is the painkiller of choice when dealing with mild to moderate pain, including fever." Your partner may be offered paracetamol to deal with pain during labour which may seem a bit like asking someone to fight a lion with a toothpick.

Her headache could be caused by stress and fear of the unknown. Unfortunately, you also have no idea what it will be like, so it may be difficult for you to help her.

Survival Tip

You may be trying to reassure your partner by "helpfully" reminding her that women have been successfully giving birth without medical support for thousands of years. This is called "free birth."

This may make her feel that she shouldn't be feeling anxious. Of course, she should; she is about to do something new that, from research, is, amongst other things, both painful and tiring.

I would remind her that you love her and are proud of how awesomely she's doing. If that is received positively, also remind her that she won't be going through this alone. She may be relieved to learn that you are there to rub her back in the wrong place and offer her toffees she doesn't want.

She will also have a team of midwives, some of whom may have been in her shoes. She will have access to the best medical knowledge and resources. As superb as all that is, it will be down to her to get her baby safely inside and outside. If that is not enough to make someone feel anxious, then I'm not sure what is. From talking to my wife, who has just walked past, the two things that helped her the most in the last few weeks of her first pregnancy were:

1. I used to bring her a pizza home (without being asked) which seems to be a key factor. I was delivering pizzas as an after-work side hustle to no doubt buy the "must have" Rolls Royce of the changing table world.
2. Giving her a cuddle with a "zero agenda" massage most nights. Just to be clear, a massage that wasn't a precursor to initiating sex and therefore viewed by her as the holy grail of massages.
3. Making her laugh, or at least trying to.

Chapter Takeaways

1. Your partner may get headaches from stress at this stage. The NHS view paracetamol as a safe pain relief for pregnant women.
2. Don't try to relieve stress by telling her that other women give birth alone in fields at night during the monsoon season. It almost certainly won't make her feel better.
3. From the best resource of knowledge I have (my wife), the best thing you can do at this point is to shower her in affection (without an agenda) and

bring her something she likes to eat or drink before she asks you to.

4. If you can make her laugh, that might help.

"When does a joke become a dad joke?

When it becomes apparent!"

- James Macdonald

Chapter 36
Week 36

What's Happening Inside At The 36-Week Stage?

Your baby is the same size as a bunch of bananas and weighs around 5-6 pounds. She or he are also about 18-19 inches in length, the same as the tyre on a Ford Mustang. Your baby's immune system, liver and kidneys are all developed now.

How Can You Support Your Partner, Baby & Yourself In Week 36?

You could create a finish line in your house, encourage your partner to shuffle through and cheer as she does. These good intentions might backfire and come across as condescending or just confusing. The 36-week mark signifies that she is now nine months pregnant, and in the home straight. As anyone who's ever run a marathon will confirm, the last 6 miles can feel harder than the previous 20. In your partner's case, the last four weeks and the labour itself might feel more physically and emotionally taxing than the previous 36 weeks.

Survival Tip

Your partner will have a 36-week prenatal appointment to establish your baby's position. If your midwife thinks it's not facing down (this is called a breech presentation), they may have to do an ultrasound to confirm that.

What Does It Mean If Our Baby Is In A Breech Presentation?

Breech births are when the baby is delivered feet or bum first. If this happens to your partner, don't panic. There's a chance your baby may get itself into the head-down position during the last four or so weeks. Approximately 1 in 25 births are breech births. Here is a brief description of the three types of breech birth.

1. **Complete breech:** baby's bum is pointing down, and their legs are folded at the knees with their feet tucked under their body as if they were doing a bomb in a swimming pool.

2. **Frank breech:** Baby's bum is pointing down, and their legs are stretched straight in front of their body. Their feet will be near their face or head.
3. **Footling breech:** is when one or both of your baby's feet point down. In this birth, their feet would be the first part of their body to be delivered.

Childbirth may be all your partner can think about, resulting in an erratic sleep pattern. Don't be surprised if you are woken at 2 am by your wife, who can't sleep and thought this would be the ideal time to paint an airing cupboard door. Be kind and try to see the humour and adventure in it all.

If you can see she's tired during the day and could do with some sleep, take the power back. Caringly wrestle the paint roller off her and send her to bed. On a positive note, this will prepare you both for the new nocturnal lifestyle you are about to embark on.

At this stage, your baby is monopolising your partner's digestive system, which can cause heartburn. If your partner has checked with her midwife first, taking antacids can help to help to relieve the discomfort. Your baby's lungs are now fully formed and ready to take that first breath. The first breath will result in its first cry. This noise is a fanfare welcoming you both to a new life of responding to his or her every demand in 2 seconds or less.

I previously mentioned Braxton Hicks (practice contractions). If your partner experiences stronger painful versions that start to come in a regular pattern, she needs to call the midwife as she's probably now in labour.

Chapter Takeaways

1. Your partner will have a 36-week appointment to check the baby is down-facing. If it's not, don't panic; doctors can use techniques to encourage them to move.
2. Your partner may be unable to sleep from anxiety related to giving birth.
3. If your partner experiences contractions (like Braxton Hicks stomach contractions) which are painful and in a regular pattern, call the midwife ASAP for advice.

"You are the best dad I could ever ask for, until you dance or sing!"

- Anonymous

Chapter 37
Week 37

Your Baby Is Now Considered Full Term!

He or she will now weigh about 4 kilograms. This is equivalent to a medium-sized pumpkin, 9 footballs or a rare breed of Italian greyhound.

What's Meconium?

This is a sticky green substance in your baby's digestive system. It will help to form the first of what will seem like a never-ending chain of poo that your baby creates for you to manage until they're about 4. The first poo I had to deal with was very dark in colour, almost tar-like. The meconium can include the fine hair (lanugo) that covered your baby earlier in your partner's pregnancy.

Survival Tip

You might find that your first official dad job is gently cleaning your baby's bum after its first poo. My daughter treated me to this moments after birth. With that in mind, I wouldn't wear any clothes you're that fond of, you may get covered in various fluids of different colours.

How Can You Support Your Partner, Baby & Yourself In Week 37?

Make sure your partner's hospital bags are packed and ready at the door. It might also be wise to do some research (often from mum blogs, ideally with a medical background) about what items they couldn't have done without.

If you have time on the way back from work, maybe practice the route you'll take once your partner starts having contractions and needs to get to the hospital. Read up on the various types of care your baby could receive after birth. The more I understood the whole process, the less anxious I felt about it.

There is the SCBU or Special Care Baby Unit. This is for babies not considered to need intensive care, often for babies born after 32 weeks of pregnancy. Our middle one had this level of care for a few days after his birth.

It can include some of the following care support:

- Their breathing or heart rate is monitored. If you're worried about the idea of this, don't be. The combination of impressive levels of medical expertise plus your partner who, from the moment your child is born, may have an innate understanding of what your baby needs.
- Providing them with more oxygen.
- They may be placed in an incubator if they have a slightly low body temperature. The last few weeks of pregnancy are when your baby develops some more of the brown fat that keeps them warm. "Brown fat" is often referred to as "good fat" and its primary function is to turn food into body heat.
- Supporting them if they have low levels of blood sugar.
- Helping to feed them. This can often be done via a tube.

If your baby needs more help, it may get admitted to the LNU or the Local Neonatal Unit. Babies who turn up between 28 and 32 weeks are often admitted to the LNU. Babies may receive the following level of medical support in the LNU:

- He or she may be given some help with breathing through their windpipe.

- Your baby may be admitted for short-term intensive care if they stop breathing for short periods (this is called apnoea).
- Your baby may get CPAP care. This stands for Continuous Positive Airway Pressure. This ventilation system delivers normal air to your child's airway at a set pressure. This care helps to keep their airway open and prevent airway blockages.
- They may be fed via a drip (tube) in a vein. The sight of pipes entering your baby may make you feel protective or emotional. This is completely understandable, but you might feel more emotional if your child couldn't access this level of care. This is undoubtedly a struggle many new parents in developing countries will face.
- If your child has had what may be described as a traumatic labour, he or she may be provided with care called "total body cooling" or whole-body hypothermia. Your baby's temperature would be carefully lowered to minimise the making of toxic substances that can cause brain injury.

The Neonatal Intensive Care Unit or NICU is the unit for the babies that require the highest level of medical care. Quite often, it's for babies born before 28 weeks or who become very unwell after birth.

Transitional Care

Sometimes you may be moved to a different hospital with a NICU before giving birth. This decision would be made when it is considered safer to transfer your baby before it is born. Babies would be cared for in a NICU if they require surgery or have had surgery, or have a severe respiratory disease that is affecting their breathing.

Once you've had some tea and toast and your partner has maybe had some surgery, you are ready to be moved to a different ward. For my wife and daughter, this meant being moved one floor down. The maternity wards seemed to be calmer; a place where the background noise was crying, snuffling babies, quiet talking, or the squelch of crocs on laminate flooring.

This is the care where your partner and baby stay together in the hospital, leaving you looking and feeling a bit redundant. I remember feeling guilty about leaving my wife, who looked like she had just returned from a war.

More qualified people could, no doubt, provide me with reasons why my suggestion that I stay to help wouldn't work. As opposed to going home to an empty house, the hours after birth seemed to be the perfect opportunity for me to step up and do some parenting. This would have allowed Mum to crawl away and find a warm, dry corner of the ward to sleep in. Dad could be left to monitor all the baby snuffling safely, knowing that medical support is only a buzzer away.

If your child needs to go into an incubator, in our son's case, to wear the pretty epic goggles that got him the nickname Buzz Lightyear, remember this is a good thing. The same should be said for tubes. Any medical support that makes your child look vulnerable might make you feel overwhelmed, and in my case, because becoming a dad also meant developing the emotions of a Disney princess.

I felt very emotional for the first few days after my daughter's arrival. Don't let this worry you, especially if you aren't normally an overly emotional man. This could be due to relief, joy or just good old-fashioned exhaustion. Your baby might need to be admitted to a special care baby unit for phototherapy to treat jaundice. Our son had some jaundice, and his breathing seemed a bit fast. Something my wife was aware of way before anyone else.

Without wanting to give my wife a big head (luckily, she probably won't read this), mums are often frustratingly accurate at knowing what children and husbands need. My wife can detect what she calls "Cat food breath"—a sign that one of our kids is coming down with some ailments days before I have any idea.

Chapter Takeaways

1. If your partner's and baby's hospital bags aren't packed and ready at the front door, do that now.
2. Go online and research the birthing experience from a dad's perspective. Knowledge is power and might help reduce anxiety around the birthing process. If all it does is reduce the number of questions you ask to exhausted and criminally underpaid medical staff, that will still be seen as a positive.

"A daughter needs a dad to be the standard against which she will judge all men."

- Bestselling Author Gregory E Lang

Chapter 38
Week 38

What's a C-Section?

Caesarean delivery or (C-section) is the name given to the surgical procedure when one or more babies are delivered through a small cut in your partner's abdomen.

There are many reasons why someone might have to, elect to, or be advised to give birth via a C-section. For example:

- If the labour isn't progressing and your partner is dangerously tired.
- If your baby is big, and to use a car analogy, it makes sense for the baby to exit via the sunroof.
- If your baby is showing signs of foetal distress.

Can The Umbilical Cord Cause Problems During Childbirth?

Yes, if the umbilical cord is too short. This happened to me during my birth. Whenever my mum tried to push, the umbilical cord would tighten and reduce my oxygen supply. This resulted in my showing signs of foetal distress. My mum was in the process of being wheeled into an ambulance to take her to another hospital for an emergency C-section when she managed to push me out.

A cord knot is when your umbilical cord gets tied. It only happens in 2% of births, and most cord knots don't cause any harm to babies while in the womb. The danger a knot in an umbilical cord poses is that it may reduce or cut off nutrients reaching your baby from the placenta.

A cord knot can, I suppose, potentially happen at any time during the pregnancy but is probably more likely to happen early in the pregnancy when the foetus is small and has more space to move around. Our eldest son had what is called a "true knot" in his cord, which my partner is convinced is why her waters broke early and he "had" to come out at 36 weeks.

How Can You Support Your Partner, Baby & Yourself In Week 38?

One symptom your partner may be experiencing this week is the frustration that it's not happened yet. 38 weeks is a long time to have to deal with swollen feet, headaches, nausea, wind, piles etc. It's also a long time to have to carry the full responsibility of growing your baby. Anything you can do this week to take her mind off her ailments or the responsibility will help. Your partner may feel some discomfort when her now "fully developed" baby moves around. These movements can result in pain in her ribs or tummy. She may also experience sharp pains in her pelvis or vagina. "Lightning crotch" is the name of these pains.

As well as sounding like something that's a hot favourite for "The National," it's also probably the last place anyone would want to see lightning!

How Does My Partner Know If The Baby's Head Is Down & Engaged?

The only way to know for sure is to have a scan. That said, your baby may be head down if your partner can feel it lower down in her bump. Your baby may also be engaged if she can feel the bottom or legs higher up your abdomen, nearer to her ribs.

Survival Tip

Don't read this out loud, but do make sure to take some time for your own mental health needs. Yes, regarding meeting your new person, your partner is doing all the heavy lifting, but your life is about to change as well, and you need some time to get your head around that.

Chapter Takeaways

1. Along with the usual suspects of swollen feet, constipation, and wind, your partner may feel frustrated and bored. Do whatever you can to keep her entertained and amused.
2. A C-section may be an option if your partner's labour isn't progressing.
3. Yes, your partner is doing the work, but you also need time to mentally prepare for becoming a dad. I've been one for over a decade now, and I still can't believe it.

"Dad, a son's first hero, a daughter's first love."

- Anonymous

Chapter 39
Week 39

How Big Is The Baby Now?

Your baby may be feeling like your partner, frustrated and that it's difficult to move. At this 39-week stage, your baby will weigh 3-3.5kg. That's like 5 courgettes or 3 pineapples.

The frustration your partner felt over the past week may have intensified. If it felt like the baby was refusing to play ball last week by not turning around, it may feel like they're playing with an actual ball this week. These often-uncomfortable movements might indicate that he or she is now "engaged" and the head is pointing down into Mum's pelvis. This can sometimes only happen right at the last moment when labour starts.

As well as feeling "pretty much done" with the waiting, your partner may feel physical symptoms like headaches. This can be due to stress, physical fatigue, or a lack of sleep. If they become severe, she should contact her midwife.

How Can You Support Your Partner, Baby & Yourself In Week 39?

If your partner gets headaches. Here are some suggestions that might help:

- Encourage her to drink at least 8 glasses of water a day.
- Help her get as much sleep as possible by moving yourself from the bed to the sofa.
- Invest in blackout blinds to ensure the room is as dark as possible.
- Buy her some earplugs, so she's not disturbed.
- What may also be effective in combating her stress is to try some meditation or maybe pregnancy yoga.

How Will We Know When The Baby Is On Its Way?

Your partner may find more vaginal discharge in her underwear than usual. This should be thick in nature, white in colour and not smell of anything in particular.

If your partner notices a slimy dollop of mucus that's either bloody or yellow, then that is what your midwife may call a "show." This "show" is the sticky stuff plugging your partner's cervix. If it comes out, this can be one of the first signs that your baby is en route.

One technique your midwife may use if your baby is over the due date is to carry out a procedure called a "sweep." If you're British and born in the 1970s or 1980s, this word may create fond memories of a grey, long-eared dog hand puppet. These two things couldn't be further apart, and if your midwife puts on a Sooty or Sweep hand puppet at any point, I would leave the room immediately.

A sweep or "membrane sweep" is when your midwife or doctor sweeps their fingers around your partner's cervix during an internal examination. This procedure should separate the membranes of the amniotic sac your baby is in from your partner's cervix. This procedure then releases a hormone called prostaglandins which can start labour.

The advice the NHS gives is to treat any of the following symptoms as an emergency and call your midwife immediately. If you're really concerned, you should escalate that and call 999 immediately:

- If your partner is bleeding from her vagina, especially if this is accompanied by stomach pains.
- If she experiences severe itching, especially at night, this could be a sign of cholestasis. This

illness is a liver condition that triggers intense itching.

- A severe headache that won't go away.
- Any vision problems (blurring a new sensitivity to light, seeing spots of flashing lights) can be a symptom of pre-eclampsia.
- Stabbing pain in the upper right area of the ribs can be a pre-eclampsia symptom.
- Persistent stomach pains.
- A high temperature above 37 degrees but without any other cold or flu-like symptoms.
- Swelling of the feet, hands or face.

Survival Tip

Knowing your limits in all areas of life is a good thing. If you are naturally queasy and prone to becoming light-headed at the mention or sight of blood, then I would advise staying at the head end during childbirth.

Chapter Takeaways

1. Your partner may get headaches caused by dehydration, lack of sleep and stress. Try to encourage her to drink lots of water and maybe try some meditation or pregnancy yoga as a way to chill out.
2. A "show" is a slimy dollop of mucus that may be

yellow or bloody. If it comes out, this can be one of the first signs that your baby is en route.

3. Any vision problems (blurring, a new sensitivity to light, seeing spots or flashing lights) can be a symptom of pre-eclampsia.

"A son is the clearest reflection of his father in the world."

- Anonymous

Chapter 40
Week 40

What Is An Assisted Birth?

An assisted birth is when your baby needs some help making its way out. The support comes from medical instruments like forceps or a suction cap. These techniques are considered safe and only used when it's considered entirely necessary. These scenarios would include if the labour wasn't progressing or if there was a critical need to deliver the baby to protect the baby's health or the mother's.

This may sound theatrical, but even during the moments of my wife's 1st labour that felt naturally dramatic, everything still felt calm and under control. I never once felt that anything was being kept from us or that our midwife wasn't completely in control of the birth.

I think midwives are probably the closest thing we have to angels in the world. During our 3 births, we were utterly blessed to have midwives who not only reassured and managed my wife but did the same for me. If it's decided that an instrument is required, your partner will often be given a local anaesthetic to number her vagina and perineum.

The perineum is the area of skin between your partner's vagina and rectum, and another obstetrician will likely need to make a cut to make the vaginal opening bigger. This procedure is called an episiotomy. If while you're reading this bit, you're also curling your toes, maybe be grateful that you were born with a penis.

If your partner's obstetrician (a doctor specialising in delivering babies) has any concerns about performing this episiotomy, they might move your partner to an operating theatre so a C-section can be carried out if needed.

If it was me, and luckily for me it wasn't, I would cement my feet firmly at the head end of the operating theatre. Seeing your partner being operated on may seem like some sort of macho medal of honour to attain. Take it from a man who had to change into his spare shorts after wetting the ones I was wearing when I fainted in a hospital. That's a medal of honour you don't need, solider.

What Is The Ventouse (Vacuum Cup)?

This medical instrument can be used if delivery isn't progressing. It involves attaching a plastic or metal vacuum cup connected by a tube to a suction device. When your partner is having a contraction, the midwife or obstetrician will gently pull to help her delivery.

If your partner is giving birth at 36 weeks or less, they may use forceps instead of the vacuum cap, as your baby's head will be softer at this point, and it could cause some damage. The forceps are smooth metal instruments that resemble the large tongs used at a BBQ. The obstetrician would carefully position the forceps around your baby's head and join them at the forceps handles. In the same way as with the vacuum cup, the doctor would gently pull the forceps during one of your partner's contractions.

One of the things that struck me the most when our daughter was born was how different it was from how child-birth is often portrayed in films.

Babies don't always come out screaming; it can take a few agonising seconds before they make any noise. From memory, that noise could often be better described as an animal-like snuffle than a cry. Our daughter came out looking a bit grey and had to have some gunk sucked out of her nose and mouth before she started making any noise On the other hand, our two boys came out making an almighty racket. If present behaviour is anything to go by, that's almost certainly because they were hungry, or it was someone else's turn to be Messi.

You will both be preoccupied with meeting your baby, but while you are, your midwife will rate your baby on the APGAR score. This comprises 5 components, and the results are rechecked after 5 minutes. This is what the APGAR score sheet might look like.

SIGN	SCORE 0	SCORE 1	SCORE 2
HEART RATE	NONE	BELOW 100 BPM	ABOVE 100 BPM
BREATHING	NONE	WEAK CRY, IRREGULAR BREATHING	STRONG CRY, REGULAR BREATHING
MUSCLE TONE	LIMP	SOME MUSCLE TONE	ACTIVE MOVEMENT
RESPONSE TO STIMULUS	NONE	GRIMACE OR WHIMPERING	CRY, SNEEZE, OR COUGH
COLOUR	PALE, BLUE	BLUE EXTREMITIES	PINK

Your baby's extremities, like their hands and feet, might appear blue. This is just because their circulation is still progressing. The rest of their body may look dark red or purple. When they start breathing, this can turn to a brighter red colour because of the increased oxygen levels.

It can take minutes before their breathing falls into a pattern, and they often resemble a cross old man who's been woken from the best nap of their life. If you have a boy, you may notice their testicles look disproportionately large. That's just a temporary thing caused by hormones and water retention.

It's not always an instant loving reunion between mother and child. Your partner may be physically exhausted and just trying to get herself through the next few minutes. According to the stats, first-time mums are usually in labour for anything from 8 to 12 hours. 2 years before giving birth, my wife completed the Brighton marathon in about 4 hours. At the time, she said it was toughest thing she had ever done. She now says that the physical and mental challenge of giving birth dwarfs a marathon and has since made that achievement more comparable to a walk in the park.

"I love my daddy. My daddy's everything, and I hope to find a man who will treat me like my dad."

- American Singer-Songwriter Lady Gaga

Chapter 41
Week 41

Shouldn't Our Baby Be Here Now?

Statistically, 75% of new mums become mums by 41 weeks and 2 days. In that 3 out of 4 mums give birth in their 41st week, your midwife may want to wait a few more days to give nature a final chance to take its course.

According to the NHS website, mums who are already mums will probably be offered a membrane sweep at their 41-week appointment.

Which Week Do Most New Babies Arrive?

The latest statistics show that 57.5% of all babies are born between 39 and 41 weeks.

Trying to process this quote below gave me a genuine headache. I had to dredge up some very old 1990s Maths on Venn diagrams.

By R Dekker – *The researchers found that 50% of all women giving birth for the first time gave birth by 40 weeks and 5 days, while 75% gave birth by 41 weeks and 2 days.*

Chapter 42
Week 42

Our First Big Day: Thursday 8th November 2012

7am - The day that would not be finishing as it began started uneventfully.

9am - I was assisting a primary teacher in a year 4 class at a primary school in East Sussex. My wife had a friend coming over for lunch, and her assignment for the day was to walk the 200-metre round trip to the shop and back to buy a pizza for lunch.

10am - I received an internal call to the year 4 classroom.

"Can Mr Macdonald please go to the school reception ASAP!"

The rest is a blur of snapshots in my mind.

Maybe 10.45am - My wife leaning forward, stabilising herself against the back of our sofa while simultaneously making a deep, rumbling animal-like groan.

Perhaps 11.30am - My wife being very unimpressed that I got us into the service lift instead of the public hospital lift. The laundry man seemed to be revelling in my misfortune.

Around Midday - My wife bursting into tears with what I can only imagine was total relief when the midwife examining her confirmed that she was 8cm dilated and, therefore, she was going to meet our daughter in a matter of hours.

Approx 16:00 - My wife insisting I turn round to face the wall in the disabled toilets when I was charged with getting her safely to and from the disabled toilets during labour.

Possibly 17:00 - My fears at the slow then fast heart rate indicating Grace may be in some distress.

My recollection of our midwife explaining to my wife that, yes, at some point, she would have to take her underwear off to give birth.

Trying to stifle my amusement when a midwife we hadn't seen before came in, looked at our clipboard, then left, and Anna turned to me and, through clenched teeth, said, "Who the f#ck was that!"

18:00 - Our lovely midwife putting on blue gloves, which was, as she said, when we would know it was about to happen.

18:07 - Finally meeting Grace. A blessing whose arrival not only turned James and Anna into Mummy and Daddy but, along with my wife, was probably my saving Grace.

"My best smile is probably when I'm holding my daughter."

- American Musician Chance The Rapper

Conclusion

If you let it, your story will naturally have all the drama, excitement, beauty and magic of a Hollywood blockbuster. While it's still clear in your mind, I urge you to try and note down your version of the day I've just described.

Even if that's 20 bullet-pointed text message you send to yourself.

It may one day help to provide you with the clarity and perspective you might need if the world seems cruel. Something warm and uncynical to read on your phone if you ever find yourself stuck in a lift or stuck and in need of a lift.

This is my first attempt at writing a book, and I'm hoping to get feedback from anyone who reads it. If you have read this book and are now a dad, I would genuinely love to hear from you.

Do you have a tip you'd like to pass on to the next wave of dads nervously trying to prepare themselves? If you'd like to get in touch, please do so at mydadmissions@gmail.com

As I mentioned early on, there is no right way to be a dad. There's just your way. Like most things, being successful is more about consistently turning up and putting in the effort.

Any dad whose child has ever asked...

"Dad, who would win in a fight between you and John Cena /Ryu/a bear?"

Know that to them, you are a hero. At least until they see you trying to change a tyre, build furniture, or dance, the illusion is then shattered.

You can be rubbish at DIY, know nothing about cars, and still be a total hero to your kids by doing some or all of the following:

- Turning up when you say you will.
- Being kind.
- Being consistent.
- Listening to them.
- Making life seem like an adventure, not a chore.
- Making fun of yourself.
- Taking ownership when you get it wrong.

- Being a glass half full, not half empty person.
- Believing in their ideas even if you don't understand them.

Doing these things will make you that person to them, and buying this book shows you're already planning to be that guy.

Good luck and let me know how it goes,

James

Helpful Resources For Dads

5 years ago, I was stressed and overwhelmed at my role as a husband and (exhausted) father of 3, not really knowing how to be the best man I could be.

Many years, pitfalls and enough flat whites to sink a battleship later, I'm a lot happier and confident and on a mission to help other dads be the best family man they can be without losing their minds through **my podcast: Dad Mind Matters: Parenting, Marriage & Mental Health For Men.**

You'll learn effective, actionable ways to deal with things like toddler tantrums, passive aggressive partners & hopefully getting more happiness & laughter into your life. You're not alone in how you feel, in Dad Mind Matters you'll find a much-needed place where you'll realise you're doing better than anyone, including you, is giving credit for.

With new bite-sized episodes every week you can learn to safely navigate family life AND have a laugh, all in the time it takes you to walk to the shop on your completely made mission to get milk.

You can listen to Dad Mind Matters podcast on your favourite platform by scanning below:

Other Useful Websites

- https://www.thedadsnet.com/
- https://www.manup.how/
- https://www.thecalmzone.net/
- https://www.nhs.uk/

Glossary & Idioms

As well as listing the words and phrases that you might not be familiar with, I have also included the idioms. I have also included a few that I have learnt along the way. If when you read my idiom you have a version, please let me know what it is, and I can credit it to you in the next book.

A

Antenatal classes: are often free courses where you will learn how to prepare yourselves for childbirth. The NHS provide a free course, but we did a course with the NCT (National Childbirth Trust), which was really good. There was a charge of £70 for a 12-hour course, but I would recommend it. The course may cover the following topics:

- How to look after your health during pregnancy.
- Specific advice on nutrition and how to manage any health issues you may encounter.
- How to write your birth plan.
- What you can expect in the later stages of your pregnancy, including the early signs of labour and how to prepare for that.

- What sort of pain relief might be available, and what might suit you best.
- Strategies to remain calm during labour and birth.

Alan Partridge: a comedy character created by a British actor called Steve Coogan. I have been mildly addicted to his work since at least 2000. He has the most loyal sense of fans, and in every place, I have worked, I have managed to sniff out a fellow Partridge Addict. If you are a man, this should be compulsory watching for you at least daily.

Anencephaly: this is a very serious birth defect where a baby is sadly born without parts of the brain and skull.

Abstain: to temporarily stop yourself from doing something you enjoy.

Aphrodisiacs: a food or drink that is thought to stimulate sexual desire.

Anaesthetist: a medical specialist who provides a substance that can reduce or remove physical pain. They are also the person your partner may be begging a midwife to try and find in the latter stages of labour.

A massive wally: is basically someone who is being a bit of an idiot. The term is friendly, almost affectionate. I often call my children "wallies" if they have put something on inside out, forgotten something, etc.

Aspirations: is another word for ambition. Like I had the ambition to train to be a stuntman so I could be in a James Bond film. At 46, that's looking more and more like it will be the one that got away.

Anesthetised: is when you have been given a substance to remove physical pain. Like paracetamol to manage a headache or alcohol to manage the stress of life.

A whitey: is when something, often drugs, alcohol, or anxiety, makes you look very pale and feel faint or sick. In extreme cases, you might be covered in a cold sweat or even pass out.

An arsenal: is a collection of weapons and military equipment. Arsenal is also a North London football club that plays in the English premier league.

Avocado brownies: are made when the butter has been substituted with avocados and the oil has been replaced with tahini.

Angus: a traditional Scottish name.

Aberdeen Angus Steakhouse: is a restaurant chain of steak houses in central London. It was also a name my wife unfairly, I think, refused to consider as a potential name for our 1st child.

A & E is the abbreviation for accident and emergency. The department in a hospital provides immediate medical help to injured people.

Abscess: is the term used to describe a collection of pus, nice!

Afterbirth: is the term used to describe the placenta and other foetal membranes that are passed by the mother from the uterus after birth.

Antibodies are blood proteins produced to attack bacteria or viruses. They are the knights in shining armour of the blood protein world.

B

Brighton Marina East Arm- Brighton Marina is an artificial marina in Brighton, UK. The east arm is the barrier on the east side.

Borat- is a satirical character created by an actor called Sacha Baron Cohen. He's the main protagonist in the film *Borat*, and the reason I'm completely unable to greet anyone in a normal way.

Blow your own trumpet is a phrase used to describe someone who is acting in a boastful, self-promoting way.

Baked Beans: is a traditional dish containing white beans in a tomato sauce. This British institution is 50% of the most celebrated student meal that goes cleverly under the name

"Beans on Toast." Canned beans are not baked but cooked through a steam process. They are then either warmed up in a pan or microwave or eaten cold from the tin while leaning against a wall after 7 pints of snake bite and black.

Babybel: is a brand of small, processed cheese products. They effectively keep a hungry, not starving child happy for 5 minutes. They are also very good at getting stuck in impossible-to-reach areas of a Citroen C5 Picasso.

Bile: blood that is produced by your liver.

Belly button: is also referred to as a naval. It's usually a human being's first-ever scar that is produced when the umbilical cord is cut after birth.

Basal body temperature is someone's coldest body temperature when they are resting, often in bed. It can predict the time of ovulation or, in my case, fool a man into thinking that his wife has thermal superpowers.

Brownie points: are an imaginary reward given for doing something kind or helpful, when trying to please.

Boobs: British slang for a women's breasts. That said, it may be used in other countries as well. Rest of the world, is that true?

Bonkers idea: a light-hearted way to say something is crazy. Therefore, in this context, it would be a crazy idea.

Bacon sandwich: a sandwich made of cooked bacon between two slices of bread. If you're new to this, you can use butter on the bread. If, like me, you cook the bacon in the microwave, you could use the bread to mop up the dripping and then lick the plate like a very happy Labrador until your wife walks into the kitchen to remind you that you aren't one.

Braxton Hicks contractions: are what is often described as a tightening sensation in your pregnant partner's abdomen. They shouldn't hurt and are often considered "practice" contractions. As a man, you are not legally allowed to call them that or refer to them in any way. I would do everything you can to never use this phrase or the word "practice" in the same sentence. They are contractions of the uterus to prepare or tone the muscles for birth.

Birth plan: is a written document of what your partner hopes to happen during labour and after the birth. You don't have to create one, but your midwife can assist if your partner wants to. I never saw my wife's 1st birth plan, but I imagine these points were on there.

Get Jimmy to frustrate me throughout by:

- Offering me a range of confectionary I don't want.
- Offering midwives mints and toffees they look like they don't want.
- Rubbing my back for too long in the same place.

- Wearing non-matching socks.

Bilateral renal agenesis is a rare condition when both kidneys don't develop properly.

C

Cuppa - British slang for a cup of white tea. This is British law. Unless they ask, a cuppa is white tea, no sugar. But here are things you must do:

- Always ask if they want sugar
- Never leave the tea bag in
- Never leave the spoon or tea bag in
- Pour the milk in first

Comms: is a short form of communication. Often used by the military or people who wish they had been in the military.

Colostrum: is the word for the first milk produced by a pregnant lady after giving birth. It's very rich in antibodies and looks sweeter than other milk, so may not require sugar.

CBT course: which stands for cognitive behavioural therapy, attempts to reduce symptoms of various mental health conditions. I was referred by my GP to do a course run by the NHS in 2010. I found it to be helpful, and it taught me various strategies to combat my anxiety surrounding intrusive thoughts.

Cholestasis of pregnancy: Intrahepatic cholestasis of pregnancy (ICP) is the common liver condition specific to pregnancy. It's a serious liver disorder that tends to develop in late pregnancy. Bile acids flows from a person's liver to their gut to help digest food. In intrahepatic cholestasis of pregnancy, the bile acids don't flow properly and build up in the body. One of the main symptoms is having very itchy skin.

Contractions: are when the uterus tightens leading up to or during labour. There are 5 types of contractions experienced during pregnancy and labour:

- **Braxton Hicks** contractions will most likely be felt in the abdomen rather than the back. They are irregular and won't increase in intensity. Apparently, they are better described as being uncomfortable as opposed to painful. They are said to subside when you lie down, go for a walk or wee.
- **Preterm labour** are contractions that happen before a pregnancy has reached full term (37 weeks). They are described as painful contractions that might be experienced more than five times in one hour. They create a hard feeling in the abdomen and menstrual-like cramps. You might have vaginal discharge, a dull ache in your lower back, pressure, and pain in your abdominal and pelvic areas.

- **Early labour contractions** are uncomfortable and can feel like you're having mild to moderate menstrual cramps. They are irregular contractions of about 30 to 45 seconds in length. They create a dull pain that radiates from the back to the front. They can make it feel like it's difficult to breathe and create pressure in the pelvic area.
- **Active labour contractions** are painful, and the green light sign that your baby is inbound. Your cervix will dilate from 4 to 10 cm at this stage. These contractions last for 50 to 75 seconds and are usually 2-3 minutes apart. This will create intense pressure and pain in the back and a strong desire to push.
- **Transition contractions** are considered the most painful and can last from 60 to 80 seconds. They are usually about 2-3 minutes apart and cause the cervix to dilate from between 7 to 10 cm.

Chromosomal anomalies: are genetic disorders which happen because of a change in chromosomes or an abnormal arrangement of chromosomes. The abnormalities can happen during the early stages of pregnancy.

A Citroen Saxo: was a supermini that was made by the French car manufacturer Citroen between 1996 and 2004.

Common knowledge: is a term for something that is or should be known by most people.

Cutting some slack: this idiom means to be less critical of someone's attitude, work, or behaviour because they are dealing with something new or challenging.

Crown to rump is the measurement of the sitting height (crown to rump) of an unborn baby.

Cheeky sod: it is a phrase that describes someone who has said or done something disrespectful or rude but has done so in a cheeky way or affectionate way.

Crunches: The crunch is another word for the abdominal exercise a sit up.

Vitamin C: which is also known as ascorbic acid, is a water-soluble vitamin found that is found in citrus and other fruits and vegetables.

Cervical mucus: is a jelly-like substance that's produced by glands in a woman's cervical canal. The mucus will appear as a discharge throughout her menstrual cycle. Your partner may notice it after wiping from going to the loo. As your partner gets closer to her time of ovulation, she may see it on her underwear.

Casualty**:** was a British medical drama series about life in a hospital.

Chorizo sausage: is a spicy sausage that consists of ground pork, garlic, and various other seasonings.

Call handlers: are the first point of human contact for

anyone calling 999 requiring immediate emergency support from one or several of the emergency services.

Café Rouge: is a French-themed restaurant chain with 30 sites across the UK.

Conceived: is the word used to describe that a sperm has met an egg, and this is the beginning of your actual pregnancy.

Cravings: is a word used to describe a powerful desire for something.

Craigslist: is a US classified ads website that has various sections where people can search for local jobs, housing, for sale, items wanted etc

Constipated: is the term used to describe your inability to have a bowel movement. This may be caused because your poo is too hard or too dry to pass without causing some pain.

Chromosome 15: is one of the 23 pairs of chromosomes in human beings.

Cleft lip: is when there is an opening in the upper lip that can extend into the nose. This opening may be on one side, both sides, or the lip's middle.

D

Dad Test: a physical or mental challenge that will no doubt be messy, expensive, stressful or all three.

Down's Syndrome, also known as trisomy 21, is a genetic disorder caused by the presence of all or part of a third copy of chromosome 21. This can result in physical growth delays, some intellectual disabilities, and characteristic facial features.

Developing a thicker skin: may be something you advise someone to do if they overreact when someone criticizes or teases them.

Dressing gown: is British for a bathrobe.

Dairy Milk chocolate: is a British brand of milk chocolate bar manufactured by the company Cadbury that's flipping yummy.

DNA: stands for deoxyribonucleic acid. It's a chemical made up of two long molecules arranged in a spiral.

Diuretic: A diuretic is any substance that increases the production of urine and makes you need to go to the loo.

Dehydration is when your body loses more fluids than you have taken in. If it's not managed, it can become a life-threatening problem.

DIY: or "Do It Yourself", is when usually against your wife's wishes, you attempt to decorate or make repairs to your home and do not employ a professional. This could also be filed under "false economy" as you often make a big mess and hire someone to sort it anyway.

Dating Scan: this is an ultrasound scan that's done between around 12 weeks of pregnancy. It has several purposes, one being to estimate your son or daughter's birth date.

Dynamically risk assessment is when you're doing the risk assessment while whatever risks you are worried about are happening in real-time.

Diaphragmatic hernia: this happens when one or more abdominal organs have moved upward into your chest through an opening in someone's diaphragm. This defect can both be present at birth or developed later in life. It's also considered a medical emergency and will require surgery to fix.

E

Episiotomy: is a surgical procedure where a small cut is made at the entrance of the vagina during childbirth. It's done to help the delivery and justify your having to take the bins out for life.

Edwards syndrome: also known as trisomy 18, is a genetic disorder which will cause delays in a child's development due to an extra chromosome 18. This can include low birth weight, abnormally shaped head, and defects in vital organs.

East Midlands: is one of the nine official regions of England. It consists of the eastern half area of England, known as the Midlands. It includes the following counties (Leicestershire, Derbyshire, some areas of Lincolnshire, Northamptonshire, Nottinghamshire, and Rutland. If someone ever asks you, "You alright, duck?" or if you might fancy a "Chip cob and a bottle of pop," they may be from the East Midlands.

Embryo: is the description used to describe an offspring that is yet to be born or hatched and is, therefore, still in the process of development.

Emergency services: is the term used to describe the organisations in the UK that would respond to and deal with emergencies. To contact them, you would call 999 in the UK.

F

Flu - (influenza) is an infection that affects the throat, nose and lungs.

Fart: is the expulsion of gas from the intestines via the anus, commonly referred to as farting.

Foetal alcohol spectrum disorder is a medical condition found in a child resulting from alcohol exposure during pregnancy. Foetal alcohol syndrome causes brain damage and growth problems.

Fosters: is a lager beer first brewed by William and Ralph Foster, two brothers who arrived in Melbourne from New York in 1886.

Folic acid: is a B vitamin found in dried beans, peas, lentils, oranges, whole-wheat, liver and asparagus. Folic acid helps the body to produce new cells and helps prevent changes to DNA that could lead to cancer.

Flipping hell: A PG-rated phrase used to express surprise or disappointment.

Foetus: the word used to describe an unborn or, depending on the species, unhatched offspring of a mammal.

Facebook Marketplace: is Facebook's classified ads section on their platform. It was launched in 2007 and, like Craigslist or Gumtree, has categories such as job opportunities, items for sale, and housing for rent or sale.

Fight or flight response is also referred to as the acute stress response. It relates to the physiological reactions that happen when you're confronted with something mentally or physically terrifying. This "fight or flight" response is triggered by the release of a cocktail of hormones that prepare your body to fight the perceived threat or run from it.

Foetal membranes- are the four membranes linked to a developing embryo or foetus. The amnion, chorion, allantois, and yolk sac.

Fingers crossed - is something people will do when they are hoping for something to happen.

Fertilised: is the word that describes what happens when an egg that's been created by a female animal or plant meets male reproductive material and grows a new individual.

G

Grab bag of crisps is a bag of crisps that, instead of being 25 grams, is twice the size at 50 grams.

Gastroschisis: is a birth defect where the baby's intestines are outside of the body due to a hole in the abdominal wall.

Gumtree: is a British-based online classified ad and community website. Like Craigslist or Facebook Marketplace, where people can offer second-hand goods and services.

***Gossip Girl*:** is an American TV series for young adults and my wife. The series is all about the lives—specifically the romantic lives—of teenagers at an elite private school in New York's Upper East side.

GP: is the abbreviation used for General Practitioner. A GP is a doctor in the community who treats patients for minor or chronic illnesses. In the case of serious conditions, they can refer you to the hospital.

Giving your 5 pence worth: or if you live stateside,

your 2 cents worth is to give someone who hasn't asked for your opinion your opinion.

Garage: is a walled and roofed structure where you keep your car. It can be attached or unattached to your home.

German measles: which is also called rubella, is a contagious viral disease. It can cause foetal malformation if a woman catches it during early pregnancy.

H

Hyperventilate: is when you breathe at an increased and abnormally fast pace. The increased amounts of oxygen ben taken in with the increased rate at which you're exhaling carbon dioxide can cause people to pass out.

Heard it on the grapevine: this phrase refers to hearing news or gathering information indirectly, quite often through gossip.

Hydrated: is when someone has drunk an adequate amount of water.

Horny: to feel sexually aroused or excited.

Hoax: means to trick or deceive someone.

Haemorrhoids: are swollen veins found in the lower area of the rectum and anus. They can cause bleeding and severe discomfort.

H&M: is the abbreviation for Hennes and Mauritz AB. It's a multinational clothing company based in Sweden.

HGC: is the abbreviation for human chorionic gonadotropin. This is the hormone that is present at high levels in early pregnancy. This hormone is what is used as a marker in home pregnancy tests.

I

Incident reference number: when you call 999 and speak to one of the emergency services, your call will have a number relating to it.

Innie: in the small dent in your stomach. It's the scar where your umbilical would have been cut.

Implantation: in the case of mammals, is when a fertilised egg or blastocyst has attached itself to the wall of the uterus at the start of pregnancy.

Immune system: is what defends your body from infections, and it's made up of a network of cells, chemicals, tissue and organs.

Intrusive thoughts: are something that most people will experience at some point in their life. They have been a considerable part of mine for as long as I can remember. For me, they can vary from mildly annoying to distressing unwanted thoughts, images, or urges that just pop into my mind. They can be very varied, but for me, they usually take the form of:

- Doubts: *"What if the bump I felt from driving over that pothole wasn't a pothole but a dog or a person?"*
  "

"What if the light wasn't green but red, and I've knocked someone down?"

- Images: *"What if the house is burning down because I left the dryer on?" "What if that sharp seashell I brushed off my foot had been in contact with a needle with AIDS on it?"*

"What if the car rolls into the road because I didn't apply the hand brake properly?"

- Impulses: *"What if I drive my car off the road?"*

"What if I call someone a highly offensive name at work or over the work radio?"

- Thoughts: *"The beds must be made, and all surfaces disinfected before I can cook myself a meal."*

"I have to put my hand under every tap in the house to check it's off before I can leave the house."

J

Jiu-jitsu: or in my case, Brazilian jiu-jitsu, is a lot more than a martial art. Jiu-jitsu is often referred to as "human chess" in that it exercises both the body and the mind. The physical benefits of jiu-jitsu are immense and well-documented. I took it up 2 weeks after my 40th birthday, and it has really helped me manage my mental health.

K

Knickers: are what the British call female underpants or panties.

Kick the habit is slang used to talk about overcoming or giving up an addiction to something that's having an unhealthy or negative impact on your life.

Knife block: is often a block of wood or another solid material with long hollow spaces designed for several sharp kitchen knives to be stored safely up to the handle.

L

Lego: is a range of plastic construction toys crafted by The Lego Group, who company based in Billund, Denmark

Large fibroids: are non-cancerous lumps or growths that develop in or on a woman's uterus. They're also known as leiomyomas and myomas.

L-shaped pillow is exactly what it says on the tin. It's a full-body pillow that is shaped in an L. It has one long side designed to run the length of someone's body with a 90-degree turn. This creates a shorter side that then fits under the shoulder, head, and neck. It's often a helpful sleeping aid during pregnancy as it supports the bump.

Lethal skeletal dysplasia is the medical term used for about 400 conditions that affect bone development, neurological function and cartilage growth.

Limb buds: are the structures formed early in a child's vertebrate limb development.

Lidl: or Lidl Stiftung & Co, is a German discount retailer chain. They have over 11,000 stores across Europe and the United States and are opening their first one on the moon this Spring. They are the perfect shop if you suddenly realise that you're running out of milk, bread, fishing rods, inflatable mattresses, or ski jackets.

Lanugo: is very fine, soft hair which covers the body of a human foetus while it's developing in the womb.

Linea nigra: that's also referred to as the pregnancy line, is a dark line that starts at your partner's pubic bone and stretches along and through her belly button during pregnancy.

Loo: is often what the British call the toilet, or if you're stateside, the bathroom.

M

Marigolds: are latex rubber gloves designed in 1947 by the UK company Marigold to protect hands when doing washing up.

Miscarriage: is the term used to describe the loss of a pregnancy during the first 23 weeks.

Missionary position: a position used in sexual intercourse where the couple lie face to face, and the woman is underneath the man.

MATB1 form: or the maternity certificate is the form a woman obtains from the government that provides her employer not only with the medical proof of her pregnancy but also when her baby is due. It is this form that allows her to claim Statutory Maternity Pay (SMP) from her employer.

Masterclass: is a specific type of class, often in one of the many creative arts like music, that's being given by an expert to a group of highly talented students.

Mr Know-It-All: Apart from being a song by the pop legend Stevie Wonder it's a way to describe someone who likes to give the impression that they are something of an expert on whatever topic is being discussed.

Maiden voyage: refers to the first of anything. For

example, if a ship is leaving port with paying passengers for the first time, it would be said to be taking its maiden voyage.

Midwife: is a specific type of healthcare provider that cares for women throughout their pregnancy, labour, birth and post-birth.

Mid-life crisis: is the term used to describe when someone (most likely male) loses their self-confidence in early middle age. They may suddenly decide to take up adrenaline-fuelled past times to breathe some excitement back into their lives.

Merlot: red wine made from the Merlot grape, which is a variety of black wine grape originally from the Bordeaux region of France.

***The Matrix*:** is a sci-fi action film that came out in 1999.

Muddy funster: is a made-up phrase I first heard on a UK comedy show that was acting out a scene from *Goodfellas* where all the swear words had been replaced with ridiculous alternatives.

Moat: a deep, wide ditch surrounding a castle, fort, or town. Usually, they would be filled with water and act as a defence against attackers.

Maltesers: British chocolate product that's manufactured by the company Mars, who make Mars bars. They were first sold in the UK in 1937, and they were originally aimed at women.

Morning sickness: is the feeling of nausea and vomiting that can often occur during pregnancy. Irrespective of its misleading name, morning sickness can happen at any time of the day or night.

Maternity leave: is the time away from work provided to a mother before and after the birth of her baby.

Maternity ward: is the area of a hospital that is allocated for the care of women and babies during their pregnancy and their childbirth.

Mucus: as the sound of the word may suggest, is a slimy substance. It's secreted by the mucous membranes and glands of human beings and animals for lubrication and protection.

N

Northern - In the context of this book, my wife has a "northern" attitude, which is a pragmatic approach. She calls a spade a spade and does not overthink a situation—the opposite of my approach to life.

Nesting: the sudden urge you may both feel to want to clean your house and get it ready for the arrival of the new member of the family. From our three experiences, it's more likely during the last few weeks of pregnancy.

NHS: stands for the UK's National Health Service. The NHS is the publicly funded healthcare system in England.

NCT: stands for the National Childcare Trust. This UK charity provides free antenatal and postnatal support and information through its nationwide network of over 300 local branches.

Nosocomephobia: is a fear of hospitals. People suffering from this phobia can experience anxiety when they visit or think about hospitals.

Nauseous: the uncomfortable feeling that you want to be sick.

O

Old wives' tale: a widely held belief that people once believed to be true is now thought to be unscientific or incorrect.

Open spina bifida: is a medical term to describe when a baby's spine and spinal cord do not develop properly, causing a gap in the spine.

OCD: is a mental health disorder I've struggled with, at least since my teenage years. It's characterised by a compulsion to repeat certain actions to try and make myself feel calm and reassured. For me, this can be lots of different things.

For example, checking the front door is locked an unspecified number of times.

Having to return to rooms to check taps are turned off. On especially bad days, this can require having to physically hold my hand underneath a tap because seeing it's turned off isn't providing enough reassurance.

It can be a compulsion to make sure lights or plug sockets are turned off for fear of starting a fire.

It's a fear that something I stood on or touched could have given me some sort of life-threatening disease.

It can be a constant feeling of anxiety that something I did or didn't do, or did or didn't say, might have directly or indirectly caused someone physical or emotional harm.

The irony is that my continuous checking is utterly counterproductive. All it does is strengthen my compulsions instead of bringing any sense of calm or reassurance.

Some days it's mildly annoying; others, it's an all-consuming, ever-present ball of anxiety that just refuses to do one.

It's worse when I'm tired or hungover and it is something my friends and family have been unbelievably patient and supportive with.

I've accepted that it's my axe to grind and that I would rather confront and discuss it in the hope that someone out there who may be dealing with similar struggles might feel slightly less crazy.

The problem I see is that due to a lack of understanding, it can come across just as being neurotic. I would never blame someone for thinking this way, but I hope that by raising the conversation about the fact that we all have mental health, we can help understand how important it is to look after it.

Offspring: is a word to describe someone's child or children.

Outie: is when you have a belly button that protrudes out rather that in.

Orgasm: is the climax of sexual excitement. It's manifested by intensely pleasurable feelings centred in the genitals. For men, this is usually experienced as an accompaniment to ejaculation:

Ointment: is a smooth substance often rubbed onto the skin for medicinal or cosmetic purposes.

Ovulation: the release of a woman's eggs from her ovaries.

Ovaries: are small, oval-shaped glands that are located on either side of a woman's uterus. They produce and store the eggs (also called an ovum).

P

Pertussis: is a highly contagious infection in the airway that primarily affects children.

Piles: is another word for haemorrhoids. They are swollen veins in the anus and lower rectum. Piles can vary in size and location, and many people with piles are unaware of them.

Perineum - The perineum for male human beings is the space between the bum hole and scrotum. For female human beings, it's the space between the anus and the vulva.

Progesterone: is a hormone that's produced by a woman's ovaries when she ovulates. Ovulation is the moment when an egg is released into the fallopian tube.

Powerwalking: or speed walking, as it is often referred to, is the act of walking with speed towards the higher end of what is deemed to be a natural walking range. This is 7 to 9 km/h.

Prescriptions - or a prescription drug (which may also be referred to as prescription medication or prescription medicine) legally require a medical prescription from a doctor to be dispensed.

Penetrative sex - is where a penis is inserted into a partner's vagina or rectum.

Pubic bone: is one of the three main bones that make up a person's pelvis. It's also called the pubis or the pelvic girdle.

Pelvic floor: is what the muscular base of the abdomen that's attached to the pelvis is called. The pelvic floor makes up the group of muscles that extends from the front of the pelvis all the way to the coccyx, which is at the back. The Pelvic floor muscle acts like a hammock in that it supports the bladder, the bowel, and the uterus inside someone's pelvis.

Pregnancy job share is when two part-time employees (*one who is pregnant*) share the workload and pay of a single full-time job employee.

Parasympathetic nervous system is part of the body's autonomic nervous system. This system is an extensive network that helps to regulate the body's involuntary processes. Things like blinking, sneezing, or yawning.

***Paw Patrol* lunch box:** *Paw Patrol* is a Canadian animated TV series that my two sons watched when they were little. A *Paw Patrol* lunch box is ultimately just a lunch box with a sticker of the *Paw Patrol* characters on it.

Pub: a pub (which is short for public house) is a place where people go to drink and socialise. It has a license to serve alcoholic drinks for people to consume while they are on the premises.

Placenta: is the flat, pancake-shaped organ that is attached to the lining of a pregnant woman's womb. It's connected to your developing baby via the umbilical cord.

Peppa Pig is an animated UK cartoon about a family of pigs aimed at pre-school-aged children.

Port in a storm is an idiom that means a place, person, or group someone may feel they can find help, refuge, or support if they are going through a difficult time.

Period: In the context of this book, a period refers to the time of a woman's menstrual cycle when she experiences bleeding from her vagina. It will usually happen every month and last for a few days.

Patau's syndrome is a serious and rare genetic disorder that is caused by someone having an extra copy of chromosome 13.

Passive aggressive: is a negative behaviour that may seem innocent accidental, or neutral but that indirectly displays an unconscious and aggressive motive. For example, "I wish I could afford a new car. Unfortunately, all my money must go on unselfish things like supporting a family."

Pre-eclampsia is a condition that can affect pregnant women, often during the second half of a women's pregnancy, so from 20 weeks onwards.

Postcode: a postal code refers to a coding system used by various countries throughout the world to simplify the processing and distribution of mail.

Q

Quintessential: is when something or someone represents the most perfect example of a specific quality.

Quentin Tarantino: is an American film director, writer, producer, and actor. His films include *Pulp Fiction, Reservoir Dogs,* and *Kill Bill.*

Quorn: the name of a village in Leicestershire, England.

R

Rhesus monkey: a small brown monkey with red skin on its face and bum native to southern Asia.

Russian dolls: or Matryoshka dolls, also known as stacking dolls, are a set of wooden dolls decreasing in size that are placed one inside another.

Richard Gere: is an American actor who started his career in the 1970s. He starred in *An Officer and a Gentleman* as well as alongside Julia Roberts in *Pretty Woman.*

Retrospect: is to look back on a past event or situation; with hindsight.

Reframing it is when you view something that happened in your past, is happening in your present, or that could happen in the future in a more positive and helpful perspective.

S

Skirting board: a wooden board that runs along the base of an interior wall. In America, you'd call this a baseboard.

Stretch marks are indented streaks that can appear on the body, breasts, hips, and buttocks. They're common in pregnant women, especially during the latter stage of pregnancy in the last trimester.

Shea butter: is a fatty substance that's harvested from the nuts of the shea tree. It is used in skin cosmetics and food.

Sofa: is the word used to describe a long, upholstered seat that has a back and arms and is at least large enough for two or more people.

Sonographer: is the name given to a healthcare professional who specialises in the use of ultrasonic imaging devices to produce diagnostic images and scans.

Salt N Vinegar crisps: are crisps (in the US, *chips*) with a salt and vinegar flavour.

Self-diagnosis: diagnosing yourself with a particular ailment or illness without consulting a medical professional.

Superdrug: is a health and beauty retailer in the UK. They used to sell pregnancy tests until my now wife bought them all in March 2012.

Stomach cramps: pain felt in the stomach due to muscle spasms.

Scatter cushions: are small cushions that are designed to be placed randomly in your home. We are still waiting for confirmation but are sure my wife still holds the Guinness World Record she's held since 2012 for the most scatter per square metre in a bedroom.

Sympathetic nervous system is part of the autonomic nervous system. The ANS is an extensive network of neurons that regulates the body's involuntary processes. The sympathetic nervous system controls aspects of the body related to its flight-or-fight response. For example, it mobilises fat reserves, increases the heart rate, and releases adrenaline so you can sprint across the living room to catch your child as they launch themselves off a coffee table or go to whack next door's sleeping Alsatian with a loo brush.

Shared workload: in the context of my marriage, "shared workload" would be any job that wasn't clearly pre-determined by gender. For example:

Boy Job	Girl Job	Shared Job
Fighting burglars	Growing people	Bedtime stories
Taking bins out	Smelling nice	Making tea
Releasing spiders back into the wild	Laughing at Dad jokes	Housework

Sudocrem: the main use of Sudocrem is for the treatment of babies' diaper (nappy) rash. But research has shown that it may help treat other conditions. For example, like gi rash if you're a 46-year-old man who often gets collar choked at Brazilian jiu-jitsu training.

Symptoms: are the physical or mental signs of an illness, injury, or condition.

Shoehorn: is to force something to be included. Alternatively, you could be forcing something into a time or space it doesn't fit into.

Sperm: is the male reproductive cell.

Shine a light: this idiom can mean to expose the truth about something or someone.

T

Triggered: feeling "triggered" isn't just something rubbing you up the wrong way. For someone who's been through a trauma, potentially a sight, smell, sound, feeling, or taste could remind them of that traumatic experience and trigger the feeling that they're experiencing the trauma all over again.

Tired and scratchy: how I describe our children at the end of a school day. The manner is tired and grumpy. Being overly unreasonable.

The lion's share means the largest part of something.

Tread carefully: means to be very careful in what you say or do.

Transparent: is when something is easy to perceive or understand.

The perfect storm: this is the idiom you could use to describe a particularly bad situation caused by several unhelpful circumstances all happening simultaneously.

Trimester: is a period of three months.

Tadpole: the tailed aquatic larva of an amphibian. At this early stage, the frog, toad, newt, or salamander would be breathing through its gills and lacking legs until the later stages of its growth.

Trust your gut refers to the idea of you trusting your feelings of intuition. Often trusting in your "gut feeling" can encourage you towards a life path that is right for you.

Tomahawk steak: also known as bone-in ribeye or tomahawk chop, is a well-marbled, rich, and thick steak with a bone still attached to it.

Time of the month refers to the time of the month when a woman has her period.

U

Ultrasound scan: also called a sonogram, is a medical procedure where high-frequency sound waves are used to create an image of part of the inside of the person's body. In the context of this book, an ultrasound scan is used to monitor an unborn baby.

Umbilical cord: the physical cord that connects the developing foetus with its mother's placenta while he or she is in the uterus. The umbilical cord's job is to transfer oxygen and nutrients from the placenta to the baby, carrying waste material away.

Uterus: or (womb) is the organ in the reproductive system of most female mammals. This includes human beings. It's the organ that accommodates an embryo and foetus during its development until its birth.

Urinate: the grown-up way of saying having a wee.

V

Vernix: or vernix caseosa, also called birthing custard, is a waxy white substance covering the skin of newborn human babies. Its purpose is thought to have a protective role during your unborn baby's development and for a few hours after his or her birth.

Vaccination: when someone is given a vaccine to help their immune system develop immunity from a particular disease. Vaccines contain a microorganism or weakened live state of an organism. The purpose of the vaccine is to then stimulate your body's adaptive immunity to stop you from getting sick from an infectious disease.

Vaginal discharge: a bodily fluid made up of fluid, cells, and bacteria. Its purpose is often to lubricate and protect the vagina. The production of vaginal discharge is not necessarily related to an underlying condition. It can also be a part of a normal menstrual cycle or due to ovulation, breast-feeding, or sexual arousal.

W

Wedding band: a ring you wear on the third finger (next to the little finger) of your left hand to indicate that you're married. It is usually forged from metal, traditionally gold or other precious metal.

Water retention: when excess fluid builds up in your body.

What 3 words: a clever digital geocoding system. It's clever because it's not limited to addresses, but what3words can help you to identify any location that is 3 metres by 3 metres or 10 by 10 feet in size.

Walkers crisps: a British snack manufacturer mainly operating in the UK and Ireland. The company is well known for the manufacture of crisps (potato chips).

Womb: (or uterus) is the name of the organ found in a woman or female mammal where her offspring are conceived and gestate before birth.

Wombat: isn't just a typo by someone trying to spell "womb" but a thing. Wombats are short, muscular marsupials that live in Australia.

Wind: is the natural movement of air or other gases relative to a planet's surface. It's also a slightly more polite way of referring to a fart.

War Horse **-** is a book by a writer called Michael Morpurgo about the relationship between a young man and his horse during the 1st World War. It has also been made into a screenplay, stage play and film.

Whooping cough: also called pertussis, is a bacterial infection of the lungs and breathing tubes. It primarily affects children and can be life-threatening.

X

X-ray: is a test using a medical machine that can produce images of structures in the body. It is often used to produce images of bones using high-energy electromagnetic waves.

Y

Ylang Ylang: or *Cananga odorata,* is a tropical tree found in the Philippines, Malaysia, Indonesia, New Guinea, the Solomon Islands, Australia, Vietnam, and Thailand. It contains essential oils with a strong floral smell that can be extracted to go into my wife's posh ylang ylang and smoky bacon shower gel.

Z

Zoom in: is the term used to describe adjusting a camera to make the object being photographed appear larger or closer and easier to inspect.

Printed in Great Britain
by Amazon

20382531R00149